OZARK METH:

A Journey of Destruction and Deliverance

by

Dick Dixon
of
Intervention Ministries

&

Laura L. Valenti

OZARK METH: A Journey of Destruction and Deliverance

Copyright © 2005 by Dick Dixon & Laura L. Valenti

All rights reserved, including the right of reproduction in whole or in part in any form without the written consent of the authors. Unauthorized use of any of the materials presented in this book is strictly prohibited.

Quotations from *Meth = Sorcery, Know the Truth* by permission of self-published author, Steve Box.

Published by:
> 3CrossPublishing
> 9757 Widmer Rd
> Lenexa, Kansas 66215
> 913.322.8629
> www.3crosspublishing.com

Layout/Design by:
> Distinctive Services, Inc.
> Springfield, Missouri 65807
> 417.889.7715

Cover Photo by:
> Eric Adams
> Lebanon, Missouri

ISBN 0-9776447-1-5

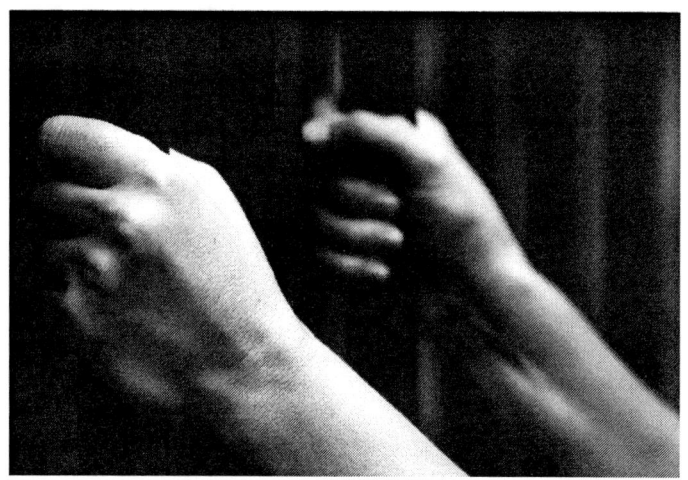

On The Inside

I never intended for it to get this bad;
I never intended my Life to get this bad…
I hated feeling like life was out of my control,
That I stayed in a constant state of mess;
That if anyone cared enough about me
They would just pluck me out of my ongoing hell…
I paced; every step soon matched
Every earth-shattering tick of the wall clock,
Each pounding reminder that life was ticking by
And I was captured in hell, going nowhere,
Walking in circles, waiting, just waiting…for what?
For a chance to escape?
I sat, stood up, and walked again.
I needed to just go in the rest room
Take a hit, ease the tension…

If they took me to jail, my work would find out...
Some would act like they never knew me...
Everyone else would just continue talking...
Maybe if they caught me though,
They could take over
Where Satan had a hold...

Within an hour, I was shooting up again.
The train rush. The hot flash.
Time passed. I was part of the fast-paced blur.
Then the brick wall.
The Sunday night slow-motion-survival-crawl
Brought me to the work week again.
At some point, I began breaking the pain of
Coming off by just staying on.
I borrowed money; I lied.
Friends and family loved me.
They had to believe me.
My bosses didn't believe me.
My mom and sister cried when they saw me.
My dad didn't cry. His eyes killed me.
They all told me they loved me.
But they stopped giving me money.
I told them they didn't love me. My dad cried.
I had new friends that loved me.

Together, I smoked, snorted, swallowed, shot up
Together, I lied, stole, and probably killed.
Together, I sacrificed parents,
Children, health, income,
Looks, sanity, morals. Freedom...
I was giving my life...to the depths of no return
I couldn't escape from what was...
...and I wouldn't care what could be...

Time ticked. Life went by.

I woke up. Still alive.
All I had left...was just the breath of me.
I was breathing.
And that is all I had left.
Everything else was gone.

With all I had left, I cried out.

And He answered,
"I am Here."

Hope
Freedom
Love

I made a phone call. They understood.

They are the Survivors—

- Users
- Families
- Dealers
- Pushers
- Pimps
- Prostitutes
- Friends
- Thieves

You reading this is not coincidence. Meth doesn't send you help—think about it.

God is bigger than—

- You
- Your problems
- Meth
- Your meth problem

When you say, "Here I am," you will hear the same.

Dedication

Dedicated to the courage of the men and women whose stories are shared here; and most importantly to the love and mercy of Jesus Christ, the One Power who is strong enough to overcome the terrible scourge known as Meth.

May God bless what is written here so that it will help all who have fallen into this trap, to find deliverance and peace in a life based on the love of the Father and The Son and The Holy Spirit. Amen.

Contents

Foreword by Dr. Mary F. Holley 11
Acknowledgments 15
We Beat Meth and You Can, Too! 18
In the Beginning 23
Chapter 1: *The Journey Begins* 29
    What's In It Really? 41
    Interview with Dr. Jon Rich 45
Chapter 2: *Acceptance Has a Price Tag* 49
    Meth World Definitions 70
Chapter 3: *Money, Sex, Power, & Paranoia* 75
Chapter 4: *Destruction* 91
    Leaving the Meth Culture the Hard Way 108
Chapter 5: *Intervention* 111
    How Were You Treated? 128
    Interview with Deputy John Young 131
    Enabling & Co-Dependence 132
Chapter 6: *Deliverance* 137
A Final Testimony 161
So What Do We Do Now? 171
    Signs & Symptoms of Meth Use 179
Appendix 1: *"On Thin Ice"* 181
Appendix 2: *Statistics: What the Numbers Tell Us* 187
About The Authors 203
Need More Help? 205

Foreword

Ozark Meth: A Journey of Destruction and Deliverance is an insightful examination of the lives of 30 recovering methamphetamine addicts. It is conducted with the rigor of a scientific study, but with none of the sterile detachment characteristics of such studies. These are real people with real struggles and real heartbreak. They have real parents and real children. They have husbands and wives. They have responsible jobs. They are your neighbors.

The addicts in this study come from all kinds of backgrounds; an incest victim and the minister's daughter, a registered nurse and a prostitute, professionals and laborers, high school drop outs and those with college degrees. There is no vaccine against methamphetamine addiction. It can happen in any family, any community.

They started young. The average age of first drug use was 12.7 years. The average age of first meth use was 20.4 years. All of them were introduced to methamphetamine by a friend. They didn't go out looking for it. It found them. Like a contagious disease, it is spread person to person, through droplets of dare, sneezes of deception, coughs of being 'cool'. They start with a little alcohol, some pot, some acid, and it gets more and more out of control. By the time we intervene, the patient is in critical condition.

This study explores the mind of the addict, the delusions and lies, the justifications and excuses, the reasons they used and the reasons they quit, and the reasons why many addicts never quit. It exposes the lie of methamphetamine, the money and sex that evaporate when you look closely, the illusion of enhanced job performance that disintegrates when the pink slip finally comes—as it always does. The feeling of being completely alive, when in actuality, they are the walking dead.

But unlike most sociological studies of its sort, this one also explores the *heart* of the addict. It reveals the fears, the pain and anger, the guilt and shame that bind and strangle them. The addicts' families are destroyed, their children abused and abandoned, and when they realize what they have done to their children, meth addicts are horrified and ashamed.

These addicts detail in their own words, the horror of hallucinations, the humiliation of sexual victimization, the loss of their jobs, their homes, their wives, their husbands, their children, and even their sanity. They expose the lies, the sickness, the loneliness and desperation of the methamphetamine lifestyle. They have lost their values, their morals, and their very identity to a substance that now possesses them.

The people in this study are the survivors. These are the people who found deliverance from addiction. They are living proof that as long as there is a pulse, there is hope. But many of their cohorts did not survive. Many more continue to struggle. Don't think the average drug addict is happy about his predicament. These people tried to quit innumerable times before they succeeded.

Every effort must be made to salvage these people from the ravages of drug addiction and restore them to their families. Rehabilitation resources, prison and jail ministry, homeless shelters and halfway houses are an immediate priority. Most addicts need twelve months of intense rehabilitation and follow up while they recover from methamphetamine. There should be a 12 step recovery support group in every town that is large enough to have a grocery store.

Foreword

But we also have to stem the tide of young children marching off the edge of the cliff. Clearly whatever we've been doing in the field of drug education has not been effective. We're starting too late and the essential message is not getting through. I wish I had a nickel for every time an inmate has told me, "Doctor, if I'd known what this drug was going to do to me, I would never have used it."

Drug education cannot be the sole responsibility of the schools. They lack the resources and moral authority to be effective in fighting this plague. If we had an infectious disease sweeping through this nation that caused this much death and destruction, the Center for Disease Control would be camped out in every high school parking lot and the entire nation would be under quarantine.

This entire nation must rise to the challenge of warning our children and citizens against this drug. Parents have to be well enough informed to be able to teach and supervise their children. Employers have a responsibility to educate their workforce. The media has an obligation to give the same level of warning and caution against meth use as they would a tornado threat. Educational public service announcements should be funded and produced, aired and talked about. Church youth workers, scout leaders, soccer coaches, every adult in every child's life must take responsibility for drug education of our youth, beginning at age eight.

Of the people represented in this study, all but two of them recognized that their relationship with Jesus Christ was crucial to their survival. They needed a Higher Power Who was willing to die for them and live within them, Someone Who would stay with them when it got down and dirty. They found that Higher Power in the Person of Jesus Christ. The current level of discrimination against Christian treatment programs in referral and funding is unwarranted in view of their success.

Law enforcement is helpless against methamphetamine. There is not enough room in all the prisons of the world to lock up every meth dealer and cook. Education is helpless against methamphetamine. The schools cannot supervise every child every hour of every day. We are the body of Christ. We are NOT helpless against methamphetamine. We can call upon the power of the Creator of this universe and pray a mighty prayer. We can and we must if we want to prevail against this evil.

—*Mary F. Holley MD*

Founder and Director, Mothers Against Methamphetamine (MAMA)
Author of *Crystal Meth: They Call it Ice* and *The High Is a Lie*

Acknowledgments

No book, especially one like this, is ever written without the help of many people, from many different walks of life. Contributions come from professional clinicians, political leaders, law enforcement experts, and persons who have suffered great pain due to the bondage of methamphetamine.

First and foremost, we want to thank the 30 individuals who shared their stories of their personal journeys down the Ozark meth road. Their candor and honest assessments of their motivations and past experiences have made this project possible and worth doing. It is with an eye to the future each has done so, in an effort to help someone else, and we are very grateful for that.

In addition, our special thanks go to:

Terry & Linda Taulbee, for their tireless efforts in conducting interviews, proofreading transcriptions, analyzing statistical data, and supporting the ideal behind this book from the very beginning;

Mary Ann Cochran and Deanna Collins, for their material and practical support which they lent to this effort on a daily basis. They are truly gifted women of God with huge hearts for others in pain;

Steve Box and Bill McLemore, who have paved the way across southwest Missouri through the *Freedom From Meth Rallies*. God is using them in a mighty way to bring deliverance to a multitude;

Dr. Jón Rich, Deputy John A. Young, and Charlie Maguire, as they all shared their expertise and experience in dealing with the plague of methamphetamine as it sweeps across our nation's heartland;

Ronda Hardt for her precious permission to share her husband's meth journey, years after his tragic death;

Dr. Paul Thomlinson and Burrell Behavioral Health for their generous collaboration in our common research projects, and finally,

Dr. Mary F. Holley, founder and director of Mothers Against Methamphetamine and fellow author, for her eloquent forward to this work and her heartfelt support, as we continue to fight this plague that has taken our land, hostage.

To each and everyone, we express our appreciation in our common battle against methamphetamine and what it does to God's own precious children.

— *Dick Dixon and Laura Valenti*

We Beat Meth...

Mary Ann

Mike

Deanna

Moses

Russell

Lynn

Danita

Karissa

Julie

Justin

Miranda

Richard

Jean

...And You Can, Too!

Michael

Shanda *Pam* *Taryn*

Russ

Debra

Tina *Duane*

Meredith *Mark*

Steve

Traci *Leilani*

Ms. Crystal Meth

I destroy homes, I tear families apart;
I take your children and that's just a start.
I'm more valued than diamonds, more precious than gold.
The sorrow I bring is a sight to behold.
If you need me, I'm easily found.
I live all around you, in your school and your town.
I live down the street or maybe next door.
I'm made in a lab, but not like you think
I can even be made under the kitchen sink,
In your child's closet, or in the woods.
If this scares you death, well, it certainly should.
I have many names, but there's one you know best.
I'm sure you've heard of me, my name's Crystal Meth.
My power is awesome. Try me, you'll see,
But if you do, you may never break free.
Just try me once, I might let you go,
But if you try me twice, I'll own your soul.
When I possess you, you'll steal and you'll lie,
You'll do what you have to, just to get high.
The crimes you'll commit for my narcotic charms
Will be worth the pleasures you'll feel in my arms.
You'll lie to your mother, you'll steal from your dad.
When you see their tears, you won't even be sad.
You'll forget your morals and how you were raised,
I'll be your new conscience. I'll teach you my ways.
I take kids from parents and parents from kids.
I turn people from God and separate friends.

I'll take everything from you, your good looks and pride,
I'll always be with you, right here by your side
You'll give up everything—your family, your home,
Your friends and your money, then you'll be all alone.
I'll take and I'll take, 'til you have nothing to give
When I'm finished with you, you'll be lucky to live.
If you try me, be warned—this is no game.
If given the chance, I'll drive you insane.
I'll ravish your body, I'll control your mind,
I'll own you completely, your soul will be mine.
The nightmares I'll give you while lying in bed,
The voices you'll hear, from inside your head.
The sweats, the shakes, the visions you'll see,
I want you to know, they're all gifts from me.
By then it's too late, and you'll know in your heart,
That you are mine, and we shall not part.
You'll regret that you tried me, they always do,
But you came to me, not I to you.
You knew this would happen, many times you were told,
But you challenged my power and chose to be bold.
You could have said No, and just walked away.
If you could live that day over, now what would you say?
I'll be your Master, you'll be my slave.
I'll even go with you when you go to your grave.
Now that you've met me, what will you do?
Will you try me or not? It's all up to you.
I can bring you more misery than words can re-tell
Come take my hand, let me lead you to hell.

—Author Unknown

This poem was given to the authors of *Ozark Meth: A Journey of Destruction & Deliverance*, from three different unconnected sources with three different names listed as the original poet, so Author Unknown is truly the case. More significant than the original author, however, is the heart-rending truth it depicts about the power of meth.

While we may not have a name for the man or woman, who penned these lines, it is apparent to all who read them, that just like the life stories you are about to read, this piece comes from the heart of someone who has traveled down the dark road of destruction that is life on methamphetamine. Whoever the original author may be, we take a moment to say 'Thank you' and 'God bless you,' in the fervent hope that you have broken free of Ms. Crystal Meth, and now live free in God's love.

In the beginning...

Once upon a time the best known illegal high in the Ozarks came as a shot from the upturned jug of Uncle Clem's 90-proof moonshine. During Prohibition in the 1920's and early 30's, the Ozark hollows were dotted with homemade copper stills, supported by whiskey drinking men. From Cat Hollow to Possum Trot Ridge and back, Ozark natives made the brew and transported it, while 'Revenoo'ers', liquor control agents of the Department of Revenue, did their best to catch them in the act of making or hauling their home made 'hooch'. If the years of Prohibition (1920-1933) taught America anything, it proved the futility of government attempts to legislate morality.

The years passed and the keepers of those copper kettle stills were replaced by secret gardeners. They were growing a little crop that was as far outside the law as moonshine ever was. This green leafy stuff looks a bit like alfalfa, but smokes entirely differently. In recent years, summer in the Ozarks brings not only tourists, but helicopters belonging to state and Federal law enforcement agencies. They search the hills and valleys and even national forest land, looking for hidden marijuana patches. Social reformers, scientists and doctors of all kinds, continue to debate the addictive aspects of marijuana and its threat or lack thereof to society. Amongst those who use it, however, and those who study the entire situation, there is no doubt that marijuana, along with alcohol, is most often the predecessor to the use of other drugs.

And today, the home grown high in the Ozarks is the story of methamphetamine. It began in the late 1980's, with a renewed interest in an old acquaintance to many in the drug culture. Methamphetamine is also known as crank, speed, crystal meth, or most simply, meth. It would soon carry another street name, "417", so named for the telephone area code of southwest Missouri.

In the early 1990's, upon his arrival from California, new Ozark resident, Bob Pailett, found Missouri meth to be more expensive and of a lesser quality than the lab product he was accustomed to on the West Coast. As a result, he set about to develop his own recipe. And in doing so, he would eventually, ravage the lives of all who would come in contact with his new and improved Ozark meth.

Visits to the local university library in search of a basic chemical formula, purchases in local hardware and farm stores, along with extensive experimentation produced a new version of Nazi meth. First used by both Hitler and his Japanese allies, this kind of methamphetamine was given to troops in decades past to produce fighting machines that could stay awake longer, run harder and survive on less food. Any serious side effects or lasting damage done to those same troops was of little concern to their leaders. There was even historical research that claimed that Hitler himself was addicted to methamphetamine.

While Pailett worked on perfecting his formula, he shared it with his new friends in southwest Missouri. In short order, they passed it on to their friends and within less than a decade, meth labs began to crop up first in rural areas, then in small towns and cities alike. At first it was just barns and out buildings, but it quickly spread to homes, mobile homes, apartments, motel rooms, and trailers. In reality, anything with a stove was fair game as far as the next meth lab site was concerned. As new formulas were developed, some of which did not require actual cooking, vehicles or anything that could hold a few beakers and containers where the lethal concoction could be brewed, was in danger of becoming a clandestine meth lab. These labs became the new #1 danger to local law enforcement, fire departments, and hospital personnel who quickly found themselves overwhelmed with meth traffic.

Children, both those belonging to the new meth cooks as well as those living in the vicinity, were also in danger. The threat of child endangerment includes the mishandling of the chemicals, the fumes from mixing and cooking, and the ever present danger of an explosion that could burn down the whole neighborhood. The industrial toxic waste site, once a distant location mentioned on the nightly news, could be growing right next door as a result of methamphetamine.

Law enforcement and medical agencies began to see the incredible damage done to human beings by this developing meth epidemic. They urged their publicity divisions and D.A.R.E. officers to incorporate meth information into their materials and classes. Doctors' offices, hospitals, and public clinics posted notices and posters warning the public of the dangers of this new drug that the meth culture touted as the poor man's cocaine. Despite their best efforts, the scourge continued to spread. Unlike past drugs, this one crossed many of the cultural barriers of American society. Meth quickly proved itself to be the new equal opportunity high that crossed gender, age, and socio-economic lines. In fact, it was an equal opportunity destroyer of life, no matter where that life might be in America.

In a March 15, 1998 article which appeared in the *Springfield News-Leader*, Bob Pailett, who had been arrested, convicted and was still on probation for his drug conviction, had relocated to northeast Texas. He stated he had no idea his meth recipe would catch fire the way it did, and that he greatly regretted his involvement.

"I wish I never started it," he said. "I would never do it again. I caused a lot of trouble for a lot of people... I hope my name is forgotten..."

According to that same newspaper article, the first clandestine meth lab was found in the Ozarks in November 1992 in Stone County. The second was discovered a few months later in Greene County and Bob Pailett was one of the persons arrested at that time. In 1997, 455 such labs were busted by law enforcement. In 2003, nearly 3000 clandestine methamphetamine lab incidents were cited in the state of Missouri alone.

Law enforcement officers are now finding meth and the attending paraphernalia on a host of affinity groups. The young, white or brown, college students, truck drivers, military men and women, factory workers, grandmothers and suburban housewives, as well as those who also regularly abuse alcohol, prescription drugs, marijuana, cocaine or even heroin—no one is immune.

Despite its rapid spread, the questions persisted amongst those who were fighting this losing battle. What is the appeal? Why were so many people becoming involved with this particular drug when they had not done so in the past? What did meth offer that the others did not?

Beginning in the fall of 2004, the staff of Intervention Ministries in Bolivar Missouri, began to ask these questions and many others, in earnest. The most logical people to ask—those who had been down this road and suffered the consequences.

A team was formed to begin a systematic research project to answer the multi-faceted question, why? The result became 30 in-depth interviews with survivors of the deadly plague known as methamphetamine. These survivors currently live in a wide multi-county area that stretches from St. Clair and Laclede Counties in the north to the Arkansas state line in the south. It runs, east to west, from the mid state region of Texas and Wright counties to the Kansas state line. In short, this area represents a greater part of the 417 area code. A few of these folks were familiar with one or two of the others, but the vast majority did not know one another. They live in Joplin, Springfield, Lebanon, Mt. Vernon, Collins, Humansville, Stockton, Aurora, and Bolivar, just to name a few of the towns involved. They did not come from one source, community resource or treatment center so the fact that their stories share several common themes is confirmation of some basic facts relative to methamphetamine use, addiction and recovery. In addition to those who have lived their whole lives here in the Ozarks, others have come to southwest Missouri from various parts of the country—Arkansas, California, Georgia, Illinois, Iowa, Louisiana, Texas, and Washington.

Two strategic sets of questions were designed. The first set, which included 56 objective short answer questions were used to collect specific answers and help the respondent to begin to chronicle their story. The in depth interview that followed, was a taped response to 54 subjective and objective questions. The last question also offered each person an opportunity to share anything else they felt was pertinent to their individual journey. All of their stories are at once, engaging, amusing, touching, frightening, heart-breaking, and in the end, with few exceptions, awesome testimonies to the power of faith and the love of Jesus Christ... their words, not ours!

Many of the answers to the questions appear to be a mixture of myth and reality. In the span of a few decades, moonshine stills have been replaced with microwaved methamphetamine. Some might say we've come a 'fur piece in these here hills' in recent years, and yet, we wonder. The myth continues, with its alluring offer, a sharpened hook to reel in the new fish. The trap of addiction closes in fast and furious. As reality sets in, many questions follow. How long does this addiction last? Can its destructive cycle be broken? What hope exists for those who want to break away? It is a grim reality that keeps many people trapped in the meth culture far too long. The greatest tragedy may be that many will deal with the after effects of this destructive addiction for the rest of their lives, as will many of their children.

These thirty survivors have been gracious enough to share their stories, and what they have suffered and learned as a result. We have done our best to put it down on paper so that hopefully others can learn the truth without having to first suffer the terrible consequences of a journey of destruction down a road marked, Ozark Meth.

Like any good travel account, we must start at the beginning...

Chapter 1

The Journey Begins...

"A journey of 1,000 miles begins with a single step."
—Confucius

The Chinese philosopher had probably never heard of methamphetamine but those who know its deceptive charms are well aware that it was that first step down the road marked Ozark Meth that led to a host of unimaginable personal losses and destructive behaviors. The newcomers are from a myriad of backgrounds and varied histories, yet most are unhappy, with who they are, at the moment of that first step. They have no real grasp of what awaits them, once they begin this journey, but the life they've heard of or seen portrayed on music videos and television, often known simply as 'partying' beckons to them. The party life is a compelling deception, with huge appeal, that offers escape from reality, whatever that may be. Despite the tearful pleas of parents and other concerned adults, such as teachers, school counselors, job supervisors, and family friends, they are determined to walk this road for themselves.

I started varsity football and baseball, my sophomore and junior years... —Russell

I am a Methodist minister's daughter... —Mary Ann

I was a prostitute in New Orleans and worked as a stripper on Bourbon Street... —Danita

I am an R.N... Pam

I was working as a private investigator... —Leilani

I was 5'9" and weighed 110 lbs my senior year in high school and kept wondering why can't I get a girlfriend? ... —Justin

I tried working at McDonald's but I didn't last 2 weeks... —Miranda

I was a hairdresser for 10 years, with a 2 week waiting list to get in to see me... —Meredith

I was 16 years in the operating room as a surgical nurse... —Jean*

* *The names of some respondents have been changed due to privacy issues.*

Without a doubt, methamphetamine is America's most democratic illegal drug of choice. Never before in America's history of drug use, has any one drug appealed to such a broad spectrum of society.

For the first half of the twentieth century, just as in previous decades, illicit drug use had been primarily confined to the poor side of town. Those in the professional community might struggle with alcohol, which was legal except for the 12 to 13 years of Prohibition in the early part of the twentieth century. On rare occasion, a doctor might find himself addicted to prescription medication. For the most part, however, addiction to illegal drugs, such as heroin, was limited to the back alleys and the fringes of society.

By the 1950's, the beat nicks, and 'cool cats' of the newest generation had begun to experiment with heroin. They mixed it with alcohol, marijuana, and even 'speed', as the early methamphetamines were known. By the early 1960's, those folks had also learned the hard way that **Speed Kills**, and they weren't just talking about going full throttle on a motorcycle. And perhaps, if society had remained the same, maintaining the ways the United States had always identified itself, life in America might have taken a different path. A little-known conflict, however, in a far corner of the world, was about to change everything we ever knew or believed about ourselves.

While US servicemen and women fought in a civil war in the Southeast Asian land of Viet Nam, many others of that same generation, rebelled, partied, struggled, and literally, dropped out of the culture in which they had been raised. While young military folks sought to ease their fear and pain in a land far from home with the rampant use of marijuana, heroin, and pills of all description, their high school and college classmates who were still living in America, protested the war. They celebrated their motto 'make love, not war', and looked to ease their pain and frustration with life, with those same drugs and more. LSD, widely known as acid, as well as the not-so-popular methamphetamine or speed, were the common drugs of choice.

While protesters marched in the streets, soldiers died in the rice paddies. The National Guard fired on college students. People who had once been dismissed as 'colored' celebrated a new Black Pride that cost many of them dearly. A handful of soldiers were court-martialed for assaults on unarmed Asian civilians. And with it all, America came as close to total cultural melt-down as it had since its own Civil War a hundred years before. The music of this new generation was as diverse as those involved in its many struggles. It simultaneously denounced the war, embraced some soldiers as heroes, encouraged all to 'love the one you're with', protested injustice of every kind, and began, little by little, to glorify drugs and those who used them.

By the mid-1970's, America was out of the war in Viet Nam, and most of the military men and women had come home. Now, along with their compatriots who had never gone to war, America faced a widespread drug culture like it had never seen before. These were not just the people who lived in the ghettos or remained discreetly outside the cultural mainstream. These were the children of Congressmen and captains of industry.

There were schoolteachers, dishwashers, doctors, lawyers, seamstresses, and mechanics, of all colors, all shades and from all parts of the nation, all experimenting with and using drugs.

Over the course of the next thirty years, the Federal government declared War on Drugs. They dumped hundreds of millions of dollars into the effort that covered everything from undercover Drug Enforcement Agency (DEA) agents, working in this country and several others, to local county sheriff's department's and their support of D.A.R.E. (Drug Awareness Resistance Education) officers, teaching American fifth graders how to 'just say No.'

Time moved on and those who grew up in that first generation of the American drug culture now had children and even grandchildren. These children, like every new generation before them, had ideas of their own. In some cases, that included thumbing their noses at Mom and Dad by experimenting with drugs, just as their parents had, even though the parents had eventually left that life behind and tried to warn their children of the inherent dangers that lurked there. For others, who had never quite made the break, of leaving the marijuana and other illegal drugs of choice in their youth, it meant their children grew up around drugs, drug paraphernalia, drug activity, and persons who used drugs. The drug culture has become enmeshed and embedded in American family life.

Twenty-first century America does not have a 'drug culture war' as much as it has become a drugged nation. And today, we find some children begin their life in drugs, by experimenting with their parents' stash. In more than a few isolated cases, parents and children end up doing drugs together.

How old were you when you first tried drugs and what did you try and why?

I was 12 and I first tried marijuana. Nobody else was around...I just got into my mom's stash. I wanted to know why my parents did it... —Karissa

I was about 6 and it was marijuana, because I'd seen my father use it... —Lonnie

I tried alcohol at 11 and meth at 13. I was selling it for my best friend... —Traci

I first tried pot when I was 11, and then alcohol. I did alcohol until I became 21 and then when it was legal, it wasn't any fun anymore... —Danita

At what age did you try meth, and how did you get it?

I was 17 and at first, I got it from my cousin... most of my family does drugs, so I mean... my ex-husband's father made methamphetamine so that's how I got it for awhile... —Shanda

At 17, I began with alcohol and then tried marijuana, then meth, then cocaine, and then heroin. Went from

using meth to selling it... my stepmother and stepbrother cooked dope, made dope... they protected me from the cooking... —Russell

Full circle indeed.

For the vast majority of addicts, however, the first time to try alcohol or illicit drugs comes in a remarkably similar fashion. Adolescence is that magical time of life, often romanticized in books and movies, when gangly suddenly long-limbed children change, over the course of a couple dozen months, into what appear to be adults, young people without restraint. The lucky ones survive the journey without any great trauma. Tragically, for many, disaster lurks in the shadows, when no one is watching closely enough. Warning signs go unrecognized or are dismissed as wild oats, teen aged angst or histrionics, or simply pass unnoticed as the adults in charge, struggle with their own battles. Parental control over children and adolescents has become ancient history in many American homes. The trend today is towards children ruling over parents rather than the reverse. Dare to discipline has been replaced by dare to inconvenience your child, for fear of being called an uncaring parent. Whatever the reason, the warnings are ignored and suddenly the enemy strikes and a child's life is forever changed.

How old were you when you first tried meth and what were the circumstances?

I tried alcohol at 14, and then marijuana and acid and at 17, meth. I got it from my friends; a couple of them brought it to me. I was at work and they made a line out in the bathroom and I went in the bathroom and snorted it. I got off work in an hour and I went and hung out with them, the boys, and just stayed up all night... —Julie

The Journey Begins

I was 17 when I first tried meth... I tried alcohol first, at age 15, rum and coke, and I drank until I was sick. I was hanging out with some friends and they said, you want to try some? ... At 17, I smoked a joint laced with PCP, and I was sick on that occasion, too... then white crosses, then meth... —Deanna

I first tried meth at 18... one of my friends had started using and I saw them using it and thought it looked cool... I just saw the way people reacted to it, and saw them actually getting their rush, and thought, I wanted to just try it to experience it... —Taryn

I was probably 15 or 16... I always ran around with older people, 5, 6, 7 years older than me... and they all partied and I thought that was the cool thing... Yeah, fitting in was a lot of it... nobody likes to be left out, you know... —Steve

I had my first drink at 13, and tried meth at 16... I just got out of juvenile hall and there is the talk...'you're big and tough, boy, what happened to you,' which is a lie. Everybody was trying it and everybody was doing it, so I felt like, hey, let me try this out, let me see if I can fit in here... —Moses

I was 22, working on a framing crew in Oklahoma, and a friend of mine had some and I tried a little... I just did it to be Superman at work or [later] at a party... —Jimmy

I had known about methamphetamine for awhile... my dad dabbled in it for a little while... but I didn't know what crank was, and I didn't know how to use it... my ex-husband and I were out with some friends of his and we got in the truck and he said, you don't mind if I try a little crank, do you? I was like, uh, all right, I guess, if you share... they put out 4 lines and he said, here, you go first, and I said, No, you go first, 'cause I didn't know how to do it... I was 23... —Meredith

There are, of course, many who also wait until a few years later. While their stories are varied, the reasons essentially boil down to the same thing—people who are not happy with who they are but are willing to look to someone or something else to complete them. They buy into what popular culture and music tell them, that the party life, a 'high' or a 'rush', will make them feel better.

My roommate's boyfriend brought it over and said, 'You wanna feel a great high?' And he injected it in my arm and I was immediately hooked... I was a big girl and the guys hadn't been really attracted to me, but this guy asked me... I was 30 when I first tried meth... —Mary Ann

I was 23 and I was out drinking and road tripping with a buddy, and he said, 'hey you want to try some meth?' and I said, yeah sure. [I didn't know what it was] and he tried to explain it, and then he said, 'you'll see' and I did... —Michael

I was 40 years old and it was becoming real evident that I had a problem [with cocaine] ... I had to leave work one day, fake being sick, go into this big lie... I go home and called a friend and they said, well, you need to get on meth. Meth will get you off the cocaine... —Jean

I was 37, my husband and I separated because he got into meth and whenever he found a 22 year old [to do drugs with], I wanted him back and I got into meth with him... it was jealousy and co-dependency... —Pam

I was 30 when I first tried meth... at 35; I started injecting it, and then selling it. He [boyfriend] was a

dealer and that was the first time I had ever seen an 8-ball... —Debra

For more than a few of the women who get involved with meth, the key to their addiction is the man they are with. Even for those who grew up with little or no exposure to drugs, which sadly often included little or no preventative drug education, a new boyfriend, who was a drug dealer, is often a one way ticket into the drug culture for a number of young women.

What was the first drug you tried and why?

I was 18 and I first tried marijuana. My husband smoked marijuana and I was married at the time. I don't think I really thought about it then. I wanted to do what other people was doing; try to be cool, you know. Fit in with the group... I never knew about drugs when I was younger. My dad was a 40 year military man. I never saw pot, cocaine, none of that until I was 18... —Debra

I tried marijuana after alcohol, and then every kind of pain pill, downer, then I went to meth... my second husband introduced me to it... —Lisa

Trying to be cool, several years later, led one of these women, now in a different relationship, down the perilous path of meth addiction. This road also eventually led to jail and prison.

The last boyfriend I got in trouble with, he was cooking and we had many fights over him cooking. I didn't want him cooking, because I knew that was one step closer to... things were bad enough already... I tried to get out of it many times, I even moved, but I come back, because I'd be worried about what was going to happen to him... —Debra

For others, tragic life circumstances, like a difficult or painful childhood open the door to drug addiction. The mistakes made in their search for self-acceptance, can be devastating.

How important was self-esteem in your decision to start using meth?

I was 18 and had just moved out of my parents' home, my adopted parents, and my dad was molesting me. I moved to [another state] with my boyfriend at the time, and his dad raped me. It was just after that, my best friend asked me to do it [meth] ... she said it would make me feel better... —Lynn

I think it was just because of my upbringing, pretty rough, so I started young, started heavy... from a military family, a lot of drinking and fighting, physical fighting... I got in a fist fight with my dad when I was probably 15, just for asking what time dinner was going to be ready... and my brothers' friends, some of them had been in Viet Nam... I was smoking pot by 14 and did acid, liquid LSD all through high school... anything to escape all that... and did a lot of cocaine by 21, 22... I did meth for the first time when I came to southwest Missouri... —Mark

I was molested as a child and I had a lot of built-up anger, that's why I started drinking, popping pills and smoking pot in the first place. I wanted to feel numb to all feelings... —Traci

I grew up in a Christian home and God was a big part of my life... I got married at 18, she was 16, and I didn't know about all the problems [we would have], but shortly after that, she cheated on me... and I was so ashamed 'cause I thought it was my fault. I thought I wasn't man enough. I wasn't a good enough provider. I was so ashamed; I couldn't talk to my God about it, because I had failed... I kept it to myself. Didn't talk to anybody... and that took me away from my religion, Bible studies, everything, and down the road to meth use... —Jimmy

As America continues to idealize the super model image, young women also continue to struggle with anorexia and bulimia and reach for any type of diet aid, including methamphetamine. For a number of young women, this adds yet another layer of self-esteem issues which then brings them to Ozark meth.

I found it was a good way to diet. I lost weight fast... —Miranda

As a society, we have long struggled with the heart-break of watching a young person leave his or her family behind, for what they perceive to be a good time and a better life than what the folks at home can offer. It is an old, old story, familiar to many. In the Bible, Jesus tells the story of the Prodigal Son. Jesus speaks of a man with two sons. The younger one decides he wants his share of his father's inheritance now, before the father has died. Unlike many modern parents, instead of getting angry or refusing his son's request, this father seems quite accommodating. He gives the boy what he asks for, and the son goes to another country, and spends all his money *with riotous living*, Luke 15:13.

Today's Prodigal sons and daughters are rarely out there on their own, and we have seen only one or two accounts of individuals who took their first steps onto the Ozark Meth road, without help, from so-called friends. Similar to Dorothy in the well-known story of the *Wizard of Oz*, as she starts down the yellow brick road, it is a trip they look forward to. With excitement and the anticipation of a new life, this trip promises more laughter and less real world tension. With rare exception, meth use almost always begins with lots of company, this being a major component of how the journey begins.

As we struggle with the many problems that drug addiction poses, both society in general as well as friends and relatives in a specific case, we often look for someone or something to blame. Sometimes, however, there are no reasons, or at least none that those looking from the outside in, can find or understand.

Still, there is some sort of skewed perception at work here. Some sort of severe denial must be involved. After all, the rational mind would never permit the contents of Ozark Meth to be put into the human body. Obviously, any substance that contains drain cleaner, lighter fluid, liquid fertilizer and many other chemicals cannot possibly be good for you!

And yet, what we need to keep in mind is that the ones who find themselves suddenly involved in the world of methamphetamine addiction often seem to have no discernible differences from those who do not wander down this disastrous detour on the path of life. That difference may be found in a better home life, one strong parent, a caring teacher or another adult who manages to let a child or young adult know that they matter, and that their life is important. At first glance, this may appear to be a small difference, and yet it is a huge difference, one that makes a life-changing turn, in terms of which road is taken.

One of the misconceptions is... there's a lot of people that do meth, that are great people, you know, and lot of them are great people when they're on meth. And some people aren't... and they can't handle it...
—Duane

The Journey Begins

We were not bad people, we were just doing drugs. We wasn't stealing, we wasn't robbing... I came home with my daughter from an open house at school [when we got busted] ... because I did these things. I was doing drugs but I still was doing the best I could at parenting... —Mark

Acceptance is huge... —Richard

Perhaps, it was best expressed by one woman who, after being off meth for 10 years, has had time to reflect on what took her down that road in the first place.

If you're not satisfied with yourself, and you're not comfortable with yourself, then you always think there is something more that you can do or be or make, and if something can make you better, or it even seems like it can make you better, you are willing to do it... I was scared as a child. I was scared of everybody and everything... I was scared to death of being myself. I wanted to be accepted and so I did what my friends were doing... —Deanna

What's in it, really?

Several of the young women we spoke with, in particular, told us that when they first tried methamphetamine, they had no idea what was in it, and that perhaps if they had known, they would never have tried it. So for clarification purposes, allow us to spell it out. The human body cannot metabolize these corrosive chemicals, and they will do great damage when they are taken into the human anatomy.

Depending upon the recipe used and there are several different recipes, methamphetamine made in clandestine labs in the Ozarks contains most of the following:

Red or Black Phosphorous — a non metallic element of the nitrogen family that once processed for industrial use is poisonous and used in the making of phosphoric acid, incendiaries and pyrotechnics, such as fireworks, safety matches, and screening smokes. Some meth cooks obtain their supply of phosphorous by using thousands of match heads. Red phosphorous is also a major component of roach and rat poisons. Black phosphorous is used as an electrical conductor in industry.

Anhydrous ammonia — a nitrogen-based fertilizer product used in large farming operations as a fertilizing agent. It is stored in large pressurized tanks and when handled incorrectly will leave serious chemical burns on bare skin. Many persons attempting to steal or transport "annie" as drug users nickname the product, have been seriously burned. Explosions during illegal transport have caused death and horrific injuries.

Several former addicts tell us that the meth made with anhydrous ammonia is much harder on the human body, than that made with phosphorous.

Lye also known as Red Devil Lye™ — a caustic, strong alkaline substance that is one of the primary ingredients in many powdered drain cleaners.

Muriatic acid — a commercial form of hydrochloric acid which is used commercially in various applications, including removing excess brick mortar, and old paint from concrete swimming pools. Hydrochloric acid in a diluted form is present in gastric juice, the stomach acid that breaks down proteins, such as meat fibers, in the human digestive tract. Hydrochloric acid is also used to etch glass and aluminum.

Lithium batteries — common batteries that can be purchased at almost any store. They are thrown into the chemical mix at a specific point, and melted into the concoction during the process.

Lantern fuel — a petroleum product, similar to kerosene, often called white gas; sometimes referred to as Coleman™ fuel, which comes from the trademark name Coleman stoves and lanterns.

Iodine crystals – a veterinary product used on the hooves of horses and cows.

Liquid drain opener, also known as Liquid Fire™— a liquid drain opener in which the primary ingredients is sulfuric acid which will burn holes in skin, clothing or other soft or porous materials.

Ephedrine — a white crystalline alkaloid extracted from a Chinese plant or more commonly today, made synthetically, and used in the form of a salt for the relief of hay fever, asthma, and nasal congestion, found primarily in cold pills. Also found in certain types of supplement blocks for animal breeding and even in some animal feed products, such as certain types of chicken feed.

Hypo phosphoric acid — the latest chemical added to the methamphetamine mix. An acid originally used to clean oil derricks; it replaces the phosphorous in the recipe and speeds up the entire process, while still producing a pure product.

Pseudoephedrine — a poisonous crystalline alkaloid that occurs, chemically speaking, with ephedrine. While it is a common ingredient in many types of cold and allergy medications, those making meth process the pills to extract the ephedrine from the pseudoephedrine for their use in manufacturing methamphetamine.

While recipes vary, most use either the anhydrous ammonia or phosphorus as the base along with the ephedrine, which is usually obtained from over the counter cold medications. At this writing, several states including Missouri, have passed laws placing these medications behind the counter, requiring their dispensation by a licensed pharmacist, requiring the buyer to show identification and sign for their purchases, as ways to control their sale to meth cooks.

At this time, the Federal government is also considering a similar law, to stop meth cooks and their helpers from simply running across state lines to the next state to buy their supplies. While the intent of such laws is laudable, it is assumed by most who have worked in and around drug addiction, for any length of time, that a new way to obtain the needed ingredients will be found or a different recipe, devised. The decrease in toxic waste sites, which pose a horrific danger to children, is also expected to result from this legislation, and that alone is worth the effort of Schedule Five legislation.

As of this writing, law enforcement officials are finding more and more methamphetamine that is being produced in foreign labs, such as Mexico and China, and then smuggled into the United States.

The Journey Begins

Interview with Dr. Jón Rich, D.O. and Chief Resident, hospital at Conroe, Texas

What does methamphetamine actually do to the body, physically?

It constricts the blood vessels, speeds up the heart, and elevates blood pressure. It also constricts the arteries and can produce kidney failure. It can kill or shut down and kill parts of several organs. It also produces heart attacks, and other heart problems, normally only seen in older people.

Things we watch for now in the Emergency Room:

- When we see 30-year-olds with chest pain or kidney failure that have no immediate cause, we ask for a urine analysis to check for drug use.

- The same with infection in the heart area. I've never seen an infection in the heart area, in a young person, who was not an IV drug user.

- Acute psychosis and schizophrenia, which can even become a permanent condition in someone with no prior history or prior family history. With a family history, meth use can definitely create problems that are likely to become permanent.

- Skin popping causes infections that we are seeing more often.

- Another new fatal condition we see is called *crack lung*, where the lungs hemorrhage as the user comes down from the high; the condition is *not* dose dependent.

- Suicidal/homicidal ideations are a common problem we see as a result of meth use.

- Most of the methamphetamine is what they call *crystal meth*. The clean stuff uses pure water, but to make it crystallize faster, many of the cooks use acetone or alcohol or something else to make it evaporate quicker.

The slower you crystallize something the purer it is.

Many of the above heath problems are also complicated by the impurities in the meth, such as lead, mercury, and acetone. Much of the cocaine for instance, is processed with leaded gasoline in the Third World. As a result, addicts are dealing with lead poisoning as well as the effects of the drugs.

What about sexual side effects?

Meth is a stimulant but there are studies that show it *increases* sexual activity. Others show it *decreases* an interest in sex.

As a stimulant, it dis-inhibits as well as energizes, so whatever a person is inclined to do, it stimulates them to do it, but even more so.

Stimulants also mess with the body's hormones. There are no studies but it is most likely a major cause of the severe acne problems we see on the face, back, and buttocks of meth users.

Without a doubt, however, the biggest health risk and problems, involve the heart. Occasional strokes are also seen due to elevated blood pressure. For a person who already has a significant health problem, like diabetes, meth use is even more dangerous.

We see occasional positive urine analysis for cocaine use, in meth users and that is dependent upon how the meth is cooked or mixed. Sometimes cocaine, heroin or other drugs are cut or mixed into it.

The Journey Begins

The US government and mass market have used amphetamines for years, which is a related and legal pharmaceutical. It is used to treat Attention Deficit Disorder (ADD), in children and adolescents and as an aid to weight loss. The Nazis and Japanese soldiers in World War II were known for using methamphetamines. Even the U.S. Army was passing out amphetamines (in the form of Ritalin®) to soldiers during Desert Storm to help keep them awake on long duty assignments.

"Methamphetamine, as it appears on the illegal market today, is extremely dangerous to everyone's health—

- to the people making it,

- to the people using it, and

- to the rest of us who have to deal with people using, who are driving, working with everything from heavy machinery to medical testing, and otherwise, going about their lives and business."

— **Dr. Jón M. Rich**
Conroe, Texas

Chapter 2

Acceptance Has a Price Tag

Every society is made up of two inseparably linked components, language and behavioral content. Together, these components are called culture. To belong to a given society, a person must know the language and the acceptable and unacceptable behaviors. There are some 6,500 languages in the world. Of course, many are closely related but even so, they represent the enormity of cultural diversification found in our world. In recent years, much has been written about cultural wars in America. Concerns such as values of family life, sanctity of life, racial equality, freedom, civil rights, sexual orientation, and drug legalization are all debated in the context of what it means to live in America today. Many of these debates are sounding boards for cultural change. Others solidify the deep appreciation for the existing American way of life, i.e., no change needed here.

Acceptance, what it is that you think is going to make you whole, and [much] of it, is going to tear you up... You know, even though meth is a dark world to live in, meth users accept each other, in the midst of their sickness, and it is very, very difficult to step away from those bonds you have made with these people. You talk about things, whenever you're on meth, and you cause relationships to be built on sharing pain... It is hard to step away because to whatever degree you know not to, when you are addicted, you love those that you are around... —Deanna

If, within a given culture, over time, behaviors develop in a specific segment of the population that are destructive to the core society, that is the definition of a counter culture. The meth user belongs to a counter culture, one opposed to the core values of American society. Much of their language usage is unacceptable to the general culture and their behaviors are counter-productive to American life.

If allowed to progress without deterrents, the core culture can be seriously damaged, if not destroyed. Meth has already reached epidemic proportions in some cities, counties, and states across America. The rapidity with which it continues to spread across the country is unprecedented and must be taken seriously, lest permanent damage result.

The problems aligned with the meth counter culture are not going to be solved by law enforcement. There are not enough courts or jails in the country; however, law enforcement is still needed. Likewise, the problems will not be solved by legislation at any level, national, state or local, yet legislation is still needed. Prevention through education is essential in protecting the public against society's bad elements, at any given time.

What will truly begin to unlock the meth problem currently impacting the American culture is an understanding of those who make up this counter culture. The best way to do that is to learn from those who have broken away, in particular, how they broke away and how they maintain their sobriety.

The new inductee to Ozark Meth wakes up in a whole new world, literally. It will take him or her awhile to realize how profoundly their world has changed.

After all, in their mind, they are simply looking for a good time, kicking back and relaxing with some friends, chilling, enjoying life, or any one of the other dozen euphemistic phrases used to cover the truth. They are now, if they were not already, a drug user.

Now, perhaps, he or she is starting to feel a little less like Dorothy of *The Wizard of Oz*, dancing down the yellow brick road on her journey to a specific destination. The new drug user begins to have a great deal more in common with Alice of Lewis Carroll's *The Adventures of Alice in Wonderland* after she tumbles down the rabbit hole. After all, in the meth world, things that once made sense, no longer do, and what used to be completely wrong, like lying to your family and friends, is now an accepted part of everyday life.

Did you hide your use from friends and family?

From my grandma... —Lynn

Yeah, I hid it in my billfold and did it in the bathroom when I wanted it... —Michael

Oh yeah, I tried to, by not going around them. I didn't see my parents for a long time, and when I did go over there, I wouldn't be high, which made it really impossible to see them, because I was doing it [meth] about every day... —Debra

Yes, I didn't tell them. I didn't talk to them. I lost all my friends. I didn't go to church anymore. I didn't call my friends. I quit my job. I quit talking to all the people that I used to talk to. No more counseling. No more outside help... —Pam

Yes. My mother suspected and confronted me, and I just lied... —Leilani

My family didn't know, but my friends, that's all my associates. My associates were my using buddies...
—Mary Ann

My parents were very naïve, to the point of craziness. They just wanted to believe I wasn't doing anything. I could come home high and they wouldn't ever say anything. I would walk in the door and be so spun I couldn't even stand still, yet they would never ask me what was wrong or anything... so we just never talked about it... —Julie

Yeah, I did for a long time. I didn't think they knew, now that I look back, I know they had to know, because I was a completely different person. I was just not myself at all, and there's no way they could not have known... I'd go to the bathroom, on a break between [hair] clients and I'd be in there 30 minutes with the boss, knocking on the door... I was just disoriented for awhile, and then I'd come out and work on clients, just spun out of my mind and I know these people thought I was nuts. But I thought I was OK. I thought I could handle it... —Meredith

From everybody except my husband... see, my kids were growing up—they were in junior high and high school—I was on the open heart surgery team and the Neuro team, two high-stress jobs. If my kids wanted to see me, they would come to my work. I would go home, my husband would complain, and I would go right back to work. I hid in work, then all of a sudden one day, my kids were gone... —Jean

I was real careful to make sure they [parents] didn't know about it, 'cause if they found out about it, I'd never hear the end of it. They couldn't handle the truth. I took a lot of pride in telling the truth, and my parents were really the only people I'll ever lie to,

because I didn't feel like they could handle the truth...
—Duane

The meth world has a whole different set of rules as well as a hierarchy of who is who. There are the so-called **Recreational Users**, also known as the weekend party people, who, like their name implies, only use on occasion or when the weekend finally arrives.

The user, you know, is somebody that can occasionally like, say for instance in the beginning, do a weekend recreational line here and there... We just did it, like on Friday nights, that was it... I don't think I knew any users... Everybody I knew were addicts... I thought we were the only ones that were recreational users... We thought we were better than everybody else... —Pam

I knew people over the years who injected drugs and I always looked down on them for doing it, you know... I thought, yeah, I'm not ever gonna do that... and then this guy I knew, he worked for a very prominent man in the local area, and held his job and I thought, well, if he can do that, maybe the stereotype of the junkie living on the street, maybe it's not that way, so maybe I could maintain my lifestyle and still [use]... —Debra

I don't think I've ever known anybody that didn't eventually get to using it [meth] on a constant, addictive basis... —Danita

Then there are the **Addicts**, who use multiple times a week, or even several times a day. Their daily or weekly habit quickly becomes a financial burden. Their habit is soon costing anywhere from $50 a day to $1000 or more a week, depending on the drug quality, the amount used, and the connections they have to get it. Most addicts advance quickly to selling and dealing meth in order to cover the cost of their addiction.

Others learn to cook, as their need increases and their financial resources are consumed.

I was what they call a functional addict... I was in that trap of, I had to have it... because I couldn't get up out of the chair [without it]. I'd have to fake an illness, you know, if I was out [of meth] and that happened a few too many times... I was so used to it, I couldn't function. I had to make sure I didn't run out, or it would be noticeable... —Duane

I was an addict before I started making [meth]... I didn't prostitute myself or anything like that. I did pawn a few things so I could start making it but I think I was to the point where I would have been a junkie... —Traci

It took my credibility away at work, even though my shop supervisor realized I was one of the best workers he had, and he always stood behind me. My fellow workers used it against me the whole time... I worked a lot of hours, like 70 or 80 hours a week. At first I did it for pleasure and then it became a way of life. Five years straight, my littlest pay check was 70 hours a week... but when I didn't have it, I was spending time, trying to get it while I was at work. I didn't have energy that I would have had, by not ever doing it, period... —Richard

And finally, there are the **Junkies**, defined by addicts as a person who will do anything, and stop at nothing to get the meth he or she needs.

A junkie, it's someone who does not have a job, a car; all they do is look for another way to get more drugs... —Justin

A junkie will lie, cheat, steal, rob, kill and destroy to get what they want... A junkie will sell everything they

own. They will rob everybody they know. The will steal anything they can get their hands on. If it ain't bolted down, they'll take it, if they can get some money for it... —Lonnie

The difference between an addict and a junkie? I call it the same thing...it got to be we couldn't function without it...it was depression... —Pam

A junkie, to me, is someone that, he could shoot up water or alcohol, just to use the needle... —Richard

And where are these folks, one might ask? They are literally all around us, as many functioning addicts continue to work regularly. In fact, several of the people we talked to always supported their habit, at least in part, by regular employment as factory line workers, in food service, landscaping, construction, janitorial, hotel housekeeping, even as health care workers! While many eventually reached a point where they could no longer maintain outside employment, the majority worked, at least intermittently.

I worked at a bank for awhile and if I needed $50, I took $50 out of the drawer. Later, when I got paid, I put $50 back in... —Miranda

I couldn't concentrate. I didn't have good judgment. I didn't care anymore. I wasn't there to do a good job. I wasn't serving God, so when... your morals are corrupt, all you're there for is a dollar now... —Pam

When I first started doing it, I had a job; I was working at a taco place... —Julie

I would get odd jobs... Eventually [I worked] as a security officer in a maximum security ward for the criminally insane... just doing meth on the side... —Mary Ann

I had a boss once, in landscaping and that's how he paid me, in meth... —Justin

Meth, when you first do it, you get an energy rush to get things done, and after that, it just got me up to normal... it just got me up to where I could function. My bosses at work were just shocked. People that have been around me for years, every day at work [college janitor] and they never knew I did it, and I'd been doing it every day... —Mark

It was affecting my job... it was digging into my paycheck and then if you counted the work I was missing and the haircuts I wasn't doing... I wasn't in control of it, I had to have it. I've never liked feeling like I was out of control, and I was. I was completely out of control... —Michael

I didn't treat customers right... I couldn't stand up because I'd get cramps in my legs and in my feet. I'd sit down. Half the time, I wouldn't show up and that's how I ended up losing my job [at the grocery store], I just wouldn't show up... —Taryn

With that in mind, it may very well be employers who need to be extra vigilant. Often when one employee begins to use, meth use can quickly spread throughout the entire firm or organization. Likewise, the new hire that discovers they have entered into a meth-structured environment, is well advised to turn and run. No job is worth that risk!

I'd prayed to God that I would get caught at work, because I knew I shouldn't be taking care of those patients, and I did... and how many others [in my part of the hospital] were using? About 6 or 7 of us, about 1/3 of the workforce... —Pam

I was working as a waitress...and most of the people there were on meth... the whole store [well known national restaurant chain] except the owner... —Taryn

I had a new job with a security firm, and I had to go miles away, early in the morning. I was tired and cranky; I'm coming down when I got the call. I knew I had to go so I dug into my stash, this really good stuff, but I lost it. I ended up driving all the way back home to find where I'd dropped it in the driveway... I was already late and they needed somebody there to watch the grounds, but by the time I got there, there were all these people there, and [my boss] ended up losing a half a million dollar account because the security was not there, so they fired my boss basically because of that [lost] contract... —Justin

You know, you got all these things going on at once, and you'll never really focus on one thing. Back then, half the plant was on meth... —Richard

I worked in a factory for 6 months, making barbecue grills and they couldn't understand how I was doing it so fast. I was shooting up in the bathroom at lunch, and I was keeping up with 18-year-old boys [when I was past 30]. I got hurt on the job and didn't want to go to the doctor, but they made me take a drug test... —Mary Ann

I was a hairdresser and when I was back on drugs [for the second time] I just didn't care. I was calling into work all the time, I've got a sick baby or I'm sick or whatever... I had a book full of clients and I just didn't show up, I just quit. I ain't coming in, and I was higher than a kite, and didn't care... —Meredith

Drug tests? There are ways... I had my daughter pee in a cup for me and I took the urine with me, concealed it, and put it in the cup... the most recent drug test I got

away with... I went to this place where you can buy pipes and drug paraphernalia and I bought a bottle of this stuff that you drink and it clears your urine of all drugs. It cost $40 and you drink it and you pee 3 times and it clears your urine. I passed my last drug test at the hospital... —Pam

Users, even the ones with jobs, soon have to find other ways to finance their habit, and that is how and why so many quickly become dealers, helpers, runners, and cooks.

Dealers run the gamut from those who begin by purchasing what they use plus some extra to sell, to help cover their costs, to those who get their supply from California or Mexico. Some are involved in major distribution operations.

We would get an 8-ball and then we'd sell some of the 8-ball in order to get back some of the money, but we dealt... we started dealing with another female dealer, we became best friends, so I became the one that would go get the drugs... hers was transported in from California and was high quality... and I would transport it home... she ended up getting busted and is in prison now for 10 years... [At the end] we were doing ice... I don't know where the ice was coming from, all I know is that this guy is getting it from a lady somewhere in southwest Missouri... so I was assuming she was cooking it... she may be getting it from California or somewhere else. She may be getting it from the A-rabs, I don't know... —Pam

I would buy an 8-ball, 3½ grams, what I didn't use, I planned on selling, keeping just a little for myself, and selling the rest, but I'd end up doing half of it... it got to where at the end, I was just asking for what's called front, I would say, can I get some on front, and then I'll pay you back when I can sell some of this, and that was just feeding my drug habit. It got to the point where the 8-ball didn't last me but a couple days and it was all me doing it. I wasn't making any money at all... —Meredith

Most users who deal in the locally made Ozark product, also "smash" what they buy. They "step on it" or "walk on it," all of which is 'drug-speak' for adding another agent to increase the volume. The white powder used to do this can be anything from a health food vitamin supplement to veterinary supply horse vitamins to baking soda. The latest reports from southwest Missouri law enforcement sources state that Mexican produced heroin has now dropped in price to a point where some are even cutting methamphetamine with heroin.

Of course, like other illegally produced drugs, there are no controls, no safety inspections, and therefore, methamphetamine can be laced with other drugs like angel dust, PCP, cocaine, or even rat poison. There is no way to tell what might be in any particular batch of illegally produced Ozark meth.

One emergency room doctor related that he often sees patients who suffer not only from the effects of whatever drug they've been using, but also from side effects of whatever has been used to cut it. This includes those dealing with the effects of lead poisoning after doing drugs produced in Third World countries where lead-based petroleum products are still used in the production of cocaine and methamphetamine!

Due to the fear of getting caught, many deal on a regular basis, with only one or two sources. Others do not have the patience for that.

The waiting game really irritates me. I really get agitated... when I have to wait for dope, I get irri-

tated... like I tell somebody hey, I need an 8-ball. All right, I'll be over there in 45 minutes. All right, 2 hours go by. You call 'em. I'll get to where... I'll wool 'em, until I get so irritated, then I'll go looking for them, and if I can't find them, then I'll go find it someplace else...
—Lonnie

And there are certainly lots of other places to look, according to those who have been in the drug life.

There never really was a time that I never could find it... My estimate? There's a meth cook for every 10 houses... I can go out to where I lived and point 'em out... there, there, and there... I've been off for 11 months, but I bet it'd take me 30 minutes to go get some... probably not even that long... —Debra

Most people will turn into a dealer at the drop of a hat...once we started cooking, we had a party of cooks every night almost, to compare dope... —Julie

In addition to actual dealers, there are also many **Runners,** or helpers, people who do favors, run errands, purchase supplies, provide places to cook and other resources, all to get their supply of methamphetamine free or nearly so.

I sold it, and I helped get supplies to make it cheaper...
—Duane

[We would] buy stuff to cook and sell it to cooks for dope. I just wouldn't have two ingredients at the same time [to keep from being arrested]... [And it went on like that] within a month after I got out of jail, for 5 more years... —Julie

I was the runner for a whole lot of dope cooks. They'd make it and I'd sell it for them. And for that, either

they gave me the money so I could buy more or they would just give me a portion... —Traci

I became what you would call a 'money man' for all these cooks around here. I would supply all their money and get 15, 16 grams off of every cook that they would do... —Russell

At 18, within a couple of months after I started using, I started selling...whenever I started distributing it, I would get all tweaked out and I would be the person who would sit and watch for people, like cops to come ... and then I began to be a runner, and I'd go get the supplies to make it with, and then the cook eventually brought me in... —Taryn

And without a doubt, in this new world, the **Cook** is the King or in rare cases, the Queen, the one with the power. This is the person who can create that which they all crave. In addition, the cook often decides who gets what and when.

How and why did you get into cooking methamphetamine?

To make sure that the good stuff was around me, 'cause I really hated buying, even a small amount and it not be any good...the devil brought it to me through somebody I knew... I went in and got the stuff and he showed me how to do it... it's easier than baking a cake... —Richard

We had a logging business, so we actually had money coming in and that's when... he started cooking, when our habit exceeded our income. It's not hard to learn... you can get on the Internet and learn and that's horrible...I got on there one night and there was a meth cooks' chat room, and I thought, how sad... —Debra

When you're cooking it, the gases and stuff that it gives off, gives you a whole different high. I was always high whenever [we were cooking]. I think cooking is an addiction in itself. I never did any anhydrous...red phosphorous was the main thing that we used...
—Taryn

Once you get arrested for it, you're a meth cook no matter where you go; you're identified as a meth cook... I used to cook at different people's houses. They gave me keys to their extra houses, to just go in and cook whenever I wanted to and I'd go where they lived and pay them [for the use of] the rental houses that they had, and then I'd clean up my mess and I'd go pay 'em in dope and they never knew I was even there, until I was done... —Danita

And the power accorded the cook often extended well beyond what was produced in the clandestine lab.

I didn't have any friends when I did drugs, especially meth, especially when I was cooking it. I had acquaintances and associates... If I saw something, I'd just take it, you know and whenever they'd ask about it, I'd say yeah, I sure did, and then they wouldn't get mad because they knew that if they got mad at me and they ran me off that I had dope and they didn't want to do that... —Danita

I was cooking dope for almost a year and a half, before I started doing dope... because there were already drugs involved in my life, whether I was doing them or not, because things were just so awful with Mom's use and my dad's use and the boyfriend's use. I was just one more person who was using... but [now] I got something everybody wants... —Karissa

Of course, theft is also a constant way of life for many in the culture of methamphetamine.

I never stole a thing... supporting my habit was dealing and of course, stolen merchandise, which I had a bunch of stuff that people would give you, $200, $300 worth of something for a ¼ gram or a ½ gram, I mean, it was just ridiculous... I'd tell myself, well, if I don't do it, somebody else will, that's how I justified it, which was not right, but that's something that goes on so much... I never sold any stolen merchandise, I had a shop, two storage units, and a house full of stuff...
—Mark

I'd steal the batteries; I'd steal the pills and whatever other little things you needed... I made it okay in my head, people is different than stores, like Wal-Mart, because they have so much money... there was no common sense to it... —Julie

I remember getting a student loan once for $10,000 and it was gone... we snorted it... I call it stealing from my parents, I would call them and they would send money, thinking it was for groceries and they'd send $200 and we'd spend $100 of it on drugs... —Pam

I did everything from petty thefts to home robberies, burglaries... —Moses

I stole money constantly... My parents used to keep cash in a drawer and I would sneak over to their house and steal $300 of the $1,000. I went to jail for gun theft... I would raid houses and steal things out of houses and sell 'em... —Miranda

I manipulated my dad into giving me $1,500 and I blew it all on meth. I told him I found a car and I was going to put a down payment on it... —Justin

I never stole dope, but the last job I had, I did steal supplies... it was a hog farm and I took blood tubes that they [addicts] used to blow out into pipes... we had

iodine and the blood tubes and you'd use those as currency. I mean, people that smoke it, they love those blood tubes... —Michael

I remember stealing money from a guy, out of his shirt pocket, who I'd just slept with, just to have money... —Mary Ann

I'd borrow things, let's put it that way [from other drug users] yeah, I mean, who are they going to turn in? What are they going to do? I'd 'borrow' their drugs, their weapons, guns, most of that stuff was stolen anyway, so we'd turn around and sell it, and then cut their dope so they wouldn't be able to track it back... —Russ

Life in a counter culture. It's not like life was at home, down on the farm, or back in the suburbs. The people are different. They appear engaging, for the most part, but the rules are different. This counter culture is much larger and more complex than they ever realized.

How many users would you say, you knew in your years of methamphetamine use? How many users, how many dealers, how many cooks?

From 100 to 200 people, using... actually I could probably buy it from 100 to 150 people at any time... —Shanda

Anywhere from 75 to 150, maybe even 250... probably about 1/6 of those were dealers, so about 20. [And I knew] about 4 cooks... —Justin

Probably 4 or 5 recreational users, they're still using to this day, [but] I've come across hundreds in my lifetime of use, including prison... I'll say about 400... —Lonnie

Acceptance Has a Price Tag

Over 100 users, and probably 15 cooks... not every cook is necessarily a dealer, my source wasn't, that's why he was probably never caught... —Duane

Over a period of years, you're talking hundreds... at least, 50 dealers, everybody was a dealer, and probably up to 10 or 12 cooks... —Miranda

Everyone I knew, hundreds of users, maybe 1,000. Hundreds of dealers, I mean like the big huge mass quantity dealers, [down] to just who does it to get free dope... the smaller ones would probably have 5 to 10 people that they'd sell to on a regular basis... I probably knew 50 different people that dealt mass quantities daily... —Julie

And yet the new meth user does his or her best to adapt and to find their place in this new world order. While many say that music and the field of entertainment had no effect on their initial decision to use methamphetamine and other drugs, most do recognize the immense impact music had on their overall use. They are emphatic about the strong influence the music had on them and their feelings that this was their new culture where they could fit in and enjoy life in a new and different way.

Did music or entertainment have an effect on you in the drug culture?

I think it had a definite pull; at least, it did on me. I think it does on a lot of other people. There's lots of negativism. Most of the stuff I listened to was songs about being high, songs about snorting up a line or shooting up or violence or gang stuff. And I just think, what you put in is what's going to come out in your life and that's what I was feeding myself... It got worse, I started listening to more of the rock, more rap, more Satanic music and then watching movies like Eminem in 8 mile, or there's a movie called Spun...lots of movies [about] drugs, heavy drug content, lots of R-rated scary movies... —Taryn

Pornography became a part of our life; it wasn't before meth... —Pam

Music sounds better, we thought it was great. [I was in a couple of rock bands] ...when you're high, you think you're fantastic... —Russ

I was an MTV freak, and I was a very plain, young girl who didn't wear makeup... it's a part of a life, the words, the parties are backed up with entertainment and music, the music goes into the depths of our souls... —Deanna

Oh yeah, it had a big effect. First of all, rap, they glorify drugs and alcohol. They glorify beating women. They glorify doing money. They glorify all that. Rock and roll glorifies most of those values, and glorifies the devil...
—Moses

Yeah, it really did. I think about that a lot. I like music. It's one of my favorite things. Rock, heavy metal, Metallica, heavy hard core bands, and now I turn on the radio and it scares me to hear one of those songs because I know that was what I listened to when I was high. That music pulled me into the dark side of things, that evil... it triggers and I don't want to hear it... —Meredith

Day after day, we'd get out of school, we'd go straight to his house and we'd smoke, and we'd sit around and listen to Led Zeppelin or whatever we wanted to listen to and we'd do that all night long... —Justin

I have a hard time [now] listening to Metallica and Pantera and things like that, the pretty heavy metal music [because] it kinda takes me back to where I was. I am very careful with my music... —Miranda

I think it has an effect on your attitude, I mean it all ties together, the mentality, the attitude. You listen to gangster music and that's the mentality that you have, that's the frame of mind, the state of mind that you live in, and you begin... that's what you believe. I mean, you know, you put the drugs in there, and they talk about the drugs, they DO the drugs, they sell the drugs, they have this I-don't-care-about-nobody mentality, so they directly tie in with one another, and not only just me explaining it, you look around, it's proven. You find me one meth user that doesn't listen to Pantera or Eminem and I'll be surprised. Find me one that listens to K-LOVE [Christian contemporary radio] and does meth, I'd be surprised... —Russell

Not everyone agreed, however. While many told us that the music world had no particular effect on them and their use of methamphetamine, others had a different view.

I don't associate rock and roll with dope, or any kind of music. In fact, I'm a blue grass fan, and I've snorted as much meth with blue grass people as I have with rock people... —Steve

And still, the party continues for a time, until little things begin to come up, unexpected things. After all, this was just supposed to be for fun, right?

I just felt like it was fun. I wasn't really worried about what anybody else would like or do or care. It was all about me. Meth just kept me awake and gave me energy... it was just a fun, party thing...[my older brother] was my idol, in the drug world... he was 4 years older than me, and he got me into all the drug *parties. I'd say my brother's name and automatically I was accepted...* —Julie

I was always big in sports, until I was a senior, and I think the partying became more important to me then, and I quit all sports and just mainly partied around... —Steve

That myth, when they say—doing it the first time, you're hooked. That's not a bad myth as far as a preventative, but I think once you go past that step, it can hurt you. It did where I was concerned because I was like, it's no big deal, I can handle that. Before I knew it, it crept up on me. I just made sure it was recreational. I didn't want to become dependent on it, but then once you start using it daily... I think anyone that's in daily use is in some kind of denial... —Duane

I didn't notice right away. I just thought I was still enjoying it, and partying with my friends. I wasn't aware at first... because pretty quick, I didn't know how to live everyday without getting high... —Deanna

It's a big lie, but you think that you can get a lot of stuff done. You even think using makes you focus on things better, but you can't stay focused 'cause you've got tons of stuff going on in your head at once... you live in denial most of the time... —Tina

Within 3 months, I lost my job and within 6 months, I lost my car... —Taryn

Over time it breaks your immune system down... when your body is first introduced to meth, you're stronger inside, [but] the more you do, the weaker you get. You build up tolerance over the years, of doing it, but you are so weak inside... [Your] body starts shutting down inside... and you don't want to come down because you're weak and you're tired and cranky and you're miserable... everybody around you is doing it, everybody that you run with does it, so it becomes your life... —Russell

I was in the party scene and I would have the marijuana and somebody else might have the acid and somebody else would have the methamphetamine, and somebody else, the cocaine and somebody else would bring the alcohol, and then we'd just all kinda share... you get as much addicted to the relationships that you have with these people. You get addicted to living in the nightmare... we would bide our time during the day and we came out at night and done all our work at night, you know, you get addicted to the whole thing... —Miranda

I started out snorting, but after years of doing it, my nose got so raw that I started putting capsules in my coffee... —Tina

I loved the burn so I enjoyed snorting it... I about cut my finger off in the mower one time. I was spinning pretty hard, pretty high, trying to get done as quick as I could so I could go play and do some more, and without thinking, I put my hand up under there... —Michael

I smoked it right out of the little crack pipe, and he's like showing me how to do it and light it and hold it and he done it real slow, just the whole ceremony of it all, basically... and my next girlfriend, her dad was a cook, so I just got it everywhere and it got me into the web, and I started finding all these people in school that did it also but they were football players, drama people, art, people going to college. I just thought that was how everybody was in that area... I ended up resorting to drugs, in order to build the reality. I wasn't an adult, [but] I'd rather not think about it soberly, because you only live once, so if you have to live your

life sober, you don't get all the extra fun of being drugged up, right? Of course, that's false, but that was my mindset, [and] it ate my soul. It took me from going in the right direction to down in this rabbit hole...
—Justin

And as the drug use continues and intensifies, the progression grows more intense. There are new aspects of this counter culture that come to light and very few of them are pleasant. This new life, these new friends and relationships, a world where one can truly fit in, is it real? Or is it merely an illusion brought on by the drugs themselves? Time will tell and the story that begins to emerge changes. It moves slowly for some, fairly quickly for most, as the new user progresses from what began as a party scene to what now looks more like a bad dream, maybe even a nightmare.

A Few Meth World Definitions

(As defined by those whose stories are told here)

8-ball — a 3½-gram measure of methamphetamine, cocaine or other drugs. The buyer often pays the going rate for 3 grams and receives the extra half gram 'free'; a $300 measure of methamphetamine in the Ozarks; a beginning to an end.

Addict — a person who abuses substance to alter mind, emotion, reality; one who has to have it, whatever 'it' may be alcohol, meth, coke, etc; someone that the drug dominates their life; someone that their life revolves around drug use, finding, buying, dealing, making, using; back then, someone else, who looked scummy, dirty, ugly, low.

Black beauties — little black happy pills; speed pills that can be bought at the convenience store.

Blunts — nickname for marijuana rolled in cigar papers. They are thicker, heavier than regular marijuana cigarettes or joints; pot rolled in a cigar leaf; also known as hog legs or fatties.

Breaking down (pills, chemicals) — preparation of pills and other chemicals before actually beginning a meth cook; also refers to the way the drug itself mixes with the cut in preparation for intravenous use. For instance, if the cut ingredient breaks down clean, then there is very little left behind, when the drug is prepared for use with a needle.

Crank — another name for methamphetamine. The name is left over from the days of speed's association with motorcyclists, who often hid their stash in the cycle's crank case.

Crystal meth — meth that is clear, and is not white, off white, yellow, brown, or purple in color like most Nazi or homemade meth, which is made in clandestine labs; looks like little crystals or bits of glass; clear, smooth pieces that look like little icicles, add water and you can watch it melt like ice in your spoon; also called glass, ice, crank, speed, zippity-do.

Ephedrine — ephedrine is a main ingredient needed to cook methamphetamine. (See "What's In It Really?" page 43)

Hot shot — a cocktail of dope, mixed with other drugs or even poisonous substances, such as paint or acids. Hot shots are used by druggers who are warring against one another, and they have been responsible for the deaths of several in the world of meth.

Ice — (see Crystal meth, above)

Jacket — prison record; the label you get from the judicial system; a person's criminal record as kept by various law enforcement agencies.

Jonesin' — wanting the drug with everything you got, all your thoughts and all your energy. When you're like that, it doesn't matter what anyone says to you.

Junkie — an addict; a needle freak; at first, a homeless person who used a needle to shoot up, but after I started shooting meth, a junkie then became someone who shot up cocaine, after I tried that, it was someone who shoots heroin. I never got to that point so therefore, I was never a junkie; anyone who will do anything, or be anything to get the drug; all my old friends.

Liquid fire — broken down dope, drawn up in the syringe, ready to be shot; "good dope" that will make you break out in an immediate sweat; one more basic meth recipe ingredient with a trademark name of Liquid Fire™. (See "What's In It Really?" page 43)

Lye — chemical used to pull (in the production of meth); active caustic ingredient in drain cleaners such as Drano™ and will cause chemical burns if dry crystals touch bare wet skin. Red Devil™ is the best known brand name of lye.

Metal dope — another name for meth made with anhydrous ammonia.

Meth whore — a girl who likes sex while high; typically, a female who will do anything to get high; someone who sleeps around for dope; anyone who sells belongings or self for drugs or parties on a constant basis; an individual, male or female, who will do *anything* to get the drug.

Off paper — getting/being off of parole or probation.

P2P dope — commercial grade chemical as well as the name of the dope made using that chemical. It was the key to the methamphetamine made in the 1960's and popularized by the motorcycle gangs. P2P dope is generally made in large labs, like those found in California.

Phosphorous, black or red — (See "What's In It Really?" page 42)

Pseudoephedrine — an ingredient in cold medications from which ephedrine is extracted to make meth. (See "What's In It Really?" page 44)

Pull — refers to various processes, in the making of methamphetamine, including breaking down cold pills to pull the ephedrine from pseudoephedrine. The different stages of these pulls is what produces the variety of color in meth from dirty or off white to yellow, purple or even cigarette ash gray; also refers to the amount of dope received from the meth cook.

Recreational user — a beginner, or weekend user; one who usually uses on weekends and occasionally at parties, although usually not for long; a weekend partier, usually Friday night, all day Saturday and coming down on Sunday to start back to work on Monday; a copout to a future addict.

Rig — refers to an addict's personal equipment, including the hypodermic used on a regular basis to inject meth or other drugs. An addict guards his or her rig, to make certain it is always available.

Smoking it off — refers to part of cooking process, where ingredient such as acetone, Coleman™ fuel or other accelerant is used to speed up the process to the finished product.

Swag — refers to goods or items traded for dope, often stolen property.

Tweaking — the state of mindlessness, when a person is totally transfixed on the task at hand and what seems like 'minutes' has actually elapsed into hours; a state of mind that comes when a person has been up for a long time and the mind is no longer working right; state of paranoia; when a person has been up for a few days and is starting to see 'bugs', can 'see the air moving', hears voices; the way one acts on meth after 4 or 5 days; what a user does after getting high, as in they 'tweak' at things until they are torn apart or destroyed.

Tweaky toys — flashlights, tools, duct tape, glue gun, soldering iron, wires, electrical tape; anything you can get your hands on, such as electronic or hand held video games; flashlights, VCR's, TV's or other appliances that can be taken apart just to put them back together again; car amps, boats, motors; colored markers and coloring books; pen and paper and all kinds of writing. Many addicts fill notebooks with 'inspired' writing, poetry, prose, song lyrics; however, when they return to the writings when no longer high, they find they make no sense whatsoever. Others also find Internet chat rooms an entertaining way to pass the hours while tweaking. Paranoia also reaches into these areas, as some report thinking that someone had "taken their notes and were [somehow] spying on them".

White crosses — over the counter pills also known as kiddy dope; ephedrine in a weaker form.

Chapter 3

Money, Sex, Power & Paranoia: The Journey Changes

The Ozarks are renowned for their natural beauty and the ability of that beauty to draw visitors from much of America, even other countries. It beckons them to come and enjoy a few restful days of soaking in nature's best. Our history bears that out in various ways and places. Harold Bell Wright's *Shepherd of the Hills* tells the story of a man who was weary of the world's values and came to what is now the area outside of Branson, Missouri, to become a simple shepherd and forget the pain he wanted to leave behind in the greater world. For more than 40 years now, local folks have been acting out the play, gleaned from the turn of the century novel, on a Branson stage, much to the delight of hundreds of thousands of tourists over the years.

Meanwhile, in the first half of the twentieth century, Hollywood's rich and famous flocked to the bath houses of Hot Springs, Arkansas for their mental and spiritual health. Those operating the hot mineral spring baths also promised many physical health benefits.

Trout fishermen have flocked to the Ozarks for the whole of the twentieth century, enjoying four Missouri state trout parks. Sportsmen of all kinds have been plying Ozark rivers, lakes, and streams for more than a century. Some enjoy guided tours of area waterways and others buy up lots, cabins, or homes for weekends and vacations. Canoeists have inundated the Ozarks for years; some to the point that the Federal government has moved in on some areas to limit the number of canoe rental operations. And for the past two decades, Branson has experienced an unending stream of tourists who come to see and enjoy the variety of shows and theme parks that offer entertainment for the entire family.

Everyone who comes to visit finds the Ozarks delightful. Nature's beauty is incomparable. The shows and other attractions are always entertaining and the prices for everything from meals to lodging are judged to be quite reasonable, especially compared to other top tourist locations around the nation. What in all of this could possibly cause a problem?

Many a visitor has been tempted to move here permanently, and some do so, buying a Mom-and-Pop resort, a gentleman's farm, or other small business, with the idea of living comfortably in such a beautiful area. However, the newcomer who has not done their homework or looked over the situation carefully from the beginning, soon discovers there is a big problem, for those who live here year round. Lower priced meals and lodging come as a direct result of lower wages for the entire area, a struggle most Ozarkers have dealt with for generations. And in the tourist industry that means many have to figure out a way to make a year's worth of living out of as little as the three months of summer!

Agricultural concerns are the state of Missouri's second biggest economic indicator, after tourism. Some Ozark land produces well, as far as crop yields and hay bales. Yet much of the land in the southern half of the state is rugged, with little topsoil, and while beautiful, it has never done a great job of producing a living. In the 21st century, the vast majority of those who still work the land in any kind of agricultural pursuit in the Ozarks do so as a second or even third source of income. They must work another full time job in a nearby city.

People continue to move to an area that they perceive as free of many of the alarming trends found in other parts of the country, such as overpriced housing, pollution, violence, overcrowded urban areas, racial tensions, and unresponsive public schools. Many also quickly find, however, that making a living in an area with low wages and low unemployment rates may not be as easy as they first thought. For others their children, the next generation, find it even more difficult. They discover an economic climate that seems to offer them little outside of work at the local factories, restaurants, or tourist attractions. Almost all wages in the area are far below what will provide them with the many baubles of the so-called good life that they see advertised on television, in popular movies and music videos. No one is suggesting that the new entrepreneurs are drug users. Certainly some are experienced in that venue. It is a fact, however that many of those in the work force that the new employers will be using as workers, are regular users.

I worked remodeling [at one of the Ozarks' biggest tourist attractions] and there were deadlines, and several work weeks where I'd work 90 hours and they never said a word, just, sometimes, they hid some of the hours, so they wouldn't get caught, I'd say... I was productive and I didn't cause no troubles or anything, but I'm operating heavy machinery and I'd been up 14 days... —Steve

The bottom line for those who live and work in the Ozarks, whether newcomer or old timer, is the same as everywhere else. Making the bottom line balance in dollars and cents is a basic requirement everywhere. In this part of the country, with depressed wages, that often, seems more difficult. Despite a relatively low cost of living, drug users must find a way to not only make a living, but also to pay for what is an ever more increasingly expensive habit.

Meanwhile, addicts who live in a fog of incredible denial are easily led to believe in illusions, including the illusion of making money by making drugs.

I had been pushing SE, the guy that I lived with, for a long time to cook because I knew we could make more money than buying it and selling it. And he was dealing in large quantities, I mean, like huge... he had good connections, and I was like, we could do this, and instead of having to buy it, we could make our own, and we could make a lot more money... —Miranda

It is one of the oldest but best lures known for reeling in the 'new fish', no matter what kind of fishing; the promise of making money, fast and easy, still sells. Suddenly, everyone wants a part of it. In this context, methamphetamine not only promises to be a great party drug, but also to provide a way to make enough money to keep the party going, or so it would seem.

... They think they can make so much money. I've never known anybody to actually make a lot of money because they end up using their own product. It's almost like they make it, just to use it. They sell it to their friends and stuff, but no one I ever knew... I don't know any meth cook, who has a home or a family, a happy family, nice stuff, maybe for a little bit, but not for long. You end up trading it off, to make more, to do more... —Debra

I didn't cook... I wasn't into getting blown up. I didn't want to get into that arena... I'd just get it, stomp on it, then sell it, double, triple the amount of stuff you get in... [But] you'd just blow all the money you have anyway, on everything else trying to fit in with the life style... —Russ

The money. We started cooking because we had no money. A big trigger for me [still] I miss the money. I went from making at least a $1,000 a night to no job at all [after jail] ... —Traci

I had a really good job at first [as a barber]... I was making $500, $600 a week and a lot of that was cash so I was just blowing money, and that's what I spent it on... it was way too much cash in the back pocket, for a person who had a habit like that... —Michael

I know I made a lot of money, [but] when you make that kind of money, you spend that kind of money and when you make that kind of money, you give away that kind of money, and whatever it takes, most of the time, you pay people in dope, close to $10,000, or $15,000... I don't even know, so many different people... I spent more time running from dope fiends than I did from the police, because there were just so many of them, and they always wanted something from you, not you, but what you had... I can tell you at the end of my journey, as I call it, I was so thankful to finally be arrested... —Danita

Without realization, the party has changed, and what was once, all for fun, has taken a much more sinister turn. Those on the meth journey are not unlike Dorothy in the *Wizard of Oz* who continues down the yellow brick road, until she unexpectedly enters a deep and foreboding forest where the trees grow so tightly together that no light seems to filter through to the forest floor. It is a much darker place than she anticipated, and so is the place where the users of methamphetamine now find themselves. It is not a place they traveled to intentionally. After all, they thought they were just "here for the party" as the song says. This party, however, is quickly turning into the line from a different song, from years before, the one where "Mama told me not to come"!

We were cooking and selling. We didn't have many people that we sold to, and it was mainly for our use. We never made any money at it really, which is a good thing, I guess... I had a business that was just barely squeaking by. I pretty much ran it into the ground and there at the end, we were just supporting ourselves off of drug sales. It was a meager existence... —Leilani

So the promise of big money is there, a promise, but little more. No one we spoke with recounted making any amount of money that lasted for any length of time. Quite the contrary. While one or two stated they made money quickly in the beginning, it did not last and just as quickly, they found themselves struggling again. There were schemes and plans aplenty on how to make big money, but there were problems, too, like Federal as well as state laws. Then, there are those who decided that the risks of drug production in other places had gotten to be too much. They, too, found themselves gravitating to a new locale, an area with less population, less overcrowding and less restrictions of all kinds, including law enforcement.

In California, you can buy an 8-ball for about $80 and in Missouri, if you don't know anybody, you're gonna pay $300, $350, [but] why take the risk of transporting it all the way back here, you know, state by state, getting an interstate transport charge? You've got a license from Missouri and you're driving, and over every state line that you pass, you're gonna get a charge in each of those states... why take that chance *when it's the same as taking a chance running around to a few stores and take the extra time and make the dope here? ... It's the difference between a simple felony that will probably get dropped to a possession charge as opposed to an interstate trafficking charge that's not going to get dropped. It's the difference between a state charge and a Federal charge. I've known people that did that kind of stuff, but they're not around any more...* —Danita

The money was a reason for some to get in deeper. They learned how to cook, as well as sell and deal, but there are other motivations as well. And some motivations hearken to the darker side of human nature.

SE used to sell me. He would sell me for drugs. He would sell me for money. There was times when he would, he would give me a pill or a drug and I would pass out and him and his friends, or whoever was at the house, and they would do whatever they did to me and I would wake up, hemorrhaging all over the bed. He used to build sex machines. He was extremely into pornography. It was just all the time. That's how we thought. It got to the point that anything we did was about sex... —Miranda

It's an aphrodisiac, 10 plus, that's what it is. It's an aphrodisiac plus, you've been to all the universities in the world, because you know everything... and you have the pornography on the TV while you're having sex over here... —Russ

I seen a lot of women, and I know a lot of strung out women that'll sleep with men for dope. They'll do whatever. One of my gay friends, he goes to the truck stops and he pimps himself out to people for money to go buy meth... —Shanda

Meth enhanced the sex... and it also [heightened] it, more often, because if you had it [meth], girls would, they'd have sex for meth... I always thought women got a bad rap on that... men, if they have a lot of sex, they're a stud; women, they're just one act away from being a tease to a whore. I always thought they got a bad rap, kind of a double standard really... —Duane

People asked me if I prostituted myself, well, I didn't get money, I got drugs, so the answer is yes... —Mary Ann

It's really embarrassing but sex plays a very big part in it, it really does... probably 8 out of 10 people will say they never ever had such good sex as they do when they're high... you lose your inhibitions. You are willing to try things that you would never ever try sober... I've seen some crazy things that people will do for drugs that I would never in a million years, think about doing, but very scary, very sick things... —Karissa

Oh, I had sex like there was no tomorrow. I didn't care who it was with... I never did sleep with anybody for drugs, but I did not have a problem, putting out... I didn't have to sleep with guys to get the drugs, but I thought I might get an extra hit if I did... I wasn't thinking about the sex, I was thinking about how much dope we were going to smoke after we were done, to celebrate or whatever... —Taryn

I became what they call a meth whore... a lot of people wouldn't think that a wife could be a whore, but that was the only time that we had sex, was under the influence of meth. And the reason why I can say I know that's what is was, because if I didn't, he became very angry at me... the sex life got dirtier and dirtier, and pornography became a part of it. It got uglier and uglier and I realize I wasn't a victim, but I thought I was...I felt forced to do things I didn't want to do... —Pam

You want to watch pornography all the time. I would leave work, when I was high on meth, and go home and watch some porno, and go back to work. Watch it at night; I can remember watching it for hours. Everybody that I know that does meth, I mean, everyone that I know that does meth watches pornography. I don't know what it is about it... it's against God. It defiles. Methamphetamine defiles everything God is about. It defiles the way a man should be with a woman. It defiles the body, being the body is the temple. It defiles the way men are supposed to love their neighbor. I mean meth is a direct insult to God. I think it's from Satan... —Russell

And if money and sex were not enough, for some it was just the euphoria of power, the power over others.

I always had drugs. I hung out with a lot of people who didn't always have drugs and I could dangle that over them. And I liked that... —Taryn

I made a little money with it, but it wasn't about money, well, maybe the cooking was a little bit... I never was into power. I never tried to use it for power over other people. Now, I know a lot of people did. They tried to use it for sex, to get people to, I didn't have sex with other women. I was married. I had a lot of opportunity, a lot of girls... I had people offer. I had girls, good-looking girls send me messages, through guys I know, 'Tell Richie, anytime he wants to go out and have a wild fling...' and I'd give it to girls I knew, like friends, but I never, when they started getting that way, I would leave, because my wife is too good of a woman to have to deal with that... —Richard

I guess it would be power, like popularity. I just did it to support my habit... —Duane

At times, I would get the thought or the feeling that I was some sort of prophet. I thought I could see into the future. I could say and do and realize things that other people didn't have a clue about... —Justin

Meth was money and then power, because as long as you had the bag of dope and the people around you didn't, you were King. That was the big power trip you got. You were in control... —Meredith

It doesn't even come and play in your mind [that you could get caught], because when you are high on meth, you can do anything. You're smart. You know everything, I mean; you're going to get away with it. You've been getting away with it so far, so what's going to happen to you now? —Russ

I felt empowered by it, so therefore, I would write notebook after notebook after notebook of just rhymes and poems and feelings... —Julie

[Meth] the feeling you got when you first used, and you wanted that back. It made you superhuman... super smart, super capable, super energized... —Pam

I was arrested for burglary... just for the joy of living on the edge... —Lisa

It's definitely about power for a man, because in the sex, he had power. If he has money, he's the power. If he can make fear, if he can put fear over someone, he has power... Now I've seen other girls that they are in it for the money and power... They've become the ones, they're the high handed ones, they're the ones doing the main cook. They hold the most dope and they've got men bowing down to them. They use men, just like the men use the women... but oh my goodness, I never had money. I was never the one with the power, I was always having to bow down to the power and for *awhile, the sex was fun and then it got to a point, where, I was afraid to say No. I was afraid not be involved in it, because of the consequences... I don't believe you can be into methamphetamine without getting into a whole new world sexually...* —Miranda

And the downward spiral continues from there. Money, sex, power, and now fear, the paranoia that effects so many who become involved with methamphetamine, takes over. The unreasonable paranoia that often crosses into insanity becomes the journey itself, a journey of fear!

You live in fear every day, is he gonna kill me today? Are the cops gonna catch me today? It's not a matter of if you'll get caught, it's just a matter of when you're gonna get caught... it's the every day running-looking-for it, trying to come up with the money to get it, it's non-stop. You look for it, you get it, then you go back out and look for it again. It's just a vicious cycle, it never stops... —Debra

I would drive but I was scared to walk from my car to the house, thinking that something was going to attack me, whether it was a person or a monster or a helicopter was going to see me or somebody was going to get a picture. I was scared of the cops. I was scared of people I'd sold bunk dope to... there were several times we'd be cooking dope and I would see police officers outside of the house. They weren't really there... or I would see UFO's in the sky. I would see hovercraft, all kinds of stuff. I had a big fascination with the sky and would think people were spying on us... —Taryn

You constantly look over your shoulder. You don't know if there's a cop behind you. My husband's big thing was the hovercraft. The hovercraft that he thought was up flying around, watching us. You will make things up. You don't think you're making them

up at the time, but your mind's making them up for you. I seen a guy one time, throwing potato chips on the floor, he was talking to something that wasn't even there. And I said, what are you doing? And he said, "I'm talking to the little green men." And I don't see anything. He's so high, he's seeing them, plain as day, and he's trying to feed them, and there's nothing there... —Karissa

I was home, where we lived out in the country, with a long driveway. There were horses and cattle in the fields [nearby] and looking out the window. I saw a farmer with a pitchfork. He was standing near a tree... and there was a horse, laying there. She was ready to have a baby, and all these people started coming around to watch her. I was on the phone to a friend, telling her... so I hung up the phone and me and my baby son, we walked down the driveway. I mean, usually you'll hallucinate for a little while and then you'll kinda snap out of it, but this wouldn't go away... [When we got there] I went to touch the baby horse it was a tree stump. There was nothing there. No horse, no farmer, no people, nothing. I had my baby in my arms and there was nothing... —Meredith

A lot of tweakers are window peekers... I would always get real mad at people for being window peekers. They're paranoid about the cops coming or what's going on outside. I was never that kind of person. If I was over at somebody's house and they were tweaking, and they'd be peeking out the windows and stuff, it would make me mad. And I didn't care if I was in their house or not, I'd let 'em know... —Lonnie

First, I started hearing things, and I would think people were talking about me. I would hear them outside of my house and I would go look and they weren't there. And I would hear someone say my name and I would go look... and after that, I started seeing things. I *would watch SE leave, and I would look out the window, and I would see him in the yard or I would see him in the shop... There were times I would just know that people were following me. I would take off in my car and I would go hide in the field for awhile, thinking people were gonna kill me. One day I stayed in a drainage ditch for like 12 hours...* —Miranda

As this life draws the user to yet a darker place, their world narrows to only a few people, only a very few things of importance.

When you get older, you start filling your life with people, baseball coaches, football coaches, friends, teachers, but as you get on meth, and your coach comes to you and says, "Russell, you look like you're losing a little weight and you're doing this, you're doing that," then you erase him from your little circle... the next thing you know this guy's gone, your friends over here are all gone, all you're left with is those little drug buddies...and when you finally wake up, it's all about me... you're all alone... —Russell

In order of importance, what were the 3 most important things in your life while you were using meth?

Using meth, power, money, and sex... —Russ

Drugs, money, power... —Karissa

I used to say, my family was always first, but that can't be the case. I'd say, meth was, what I had at the time, was most important, and the second thing, I always thought about was where am I going to get it, when I run out, and then I'd say, down close to the bottom was the health and welfare of my family... —Jimmy

Buying chemicals, transportation to go get chemicals, and where I was gonna cook it at... —Danita

Meth, sex, meth... —Mary Ann

Having it, just having the dope, having the money and being high... —Lynn

Getting high, hanging out with friends, and pornography, which was the big thing when I was high... —Russell

Getting stuff to make drugs, finding the ingredients, buying it, doing it... —Mark

Getting drugs, making drugs, doing drugs... —Leilani

How much I had left and when I ran out where was I going to get some more, and did I have any clean needles... —Meredith

To always have drugs, to always have money, to always have alcohol... —Mike

Drugs, getting drugs, using drugs, coming up with money to get more... —Danita

Dope, money, sex... —Lisa

Get my dope, get my dope, get my dope... —Deanna

And now the tight little circle has come down to this. Without meth, there is no life. For so many, methamphetamine and all that it entails, has become life, their only life, and others who use the drugs, their only associates. The journey continues, but not to a place that anyone wants to go.

My whole life revolved around the drug and I eventually started making it. I got to the point when I stopped making it, that I had nothing at all. When I went to jail, I lost my house, my car, everything...
—Traci

Chapter 4

Destruction

"Enter through the narrow gate. For wide is the gate and broad is the road that leads to destruction, and many enter through it. But small is the gate and narrow the road that leads to life, and only a few find it."
—Jesus Christ, Matthew 7:13-14

As a society, we tend to forget our history, especially the unpleasant or unattractive parts. When we look back on the history of America, especially the mid-section of the country, we tend to remember the humor and innocence of Mark Twain's stories about life on the Mississippi, the courage and strength of the original settlers, many of whom walked hundreds of miles to get here or to continue even further across the continent. We often choose not to remember the conflicts, the divided loyalties, and the violent confrontations that occasionally resulted.

Springfield, Missouri, for instance, does not celebrate the fact that Bill Hickok—later nicknamed 'Wild Bill'—is credited (or blamed) for the first argument settled by a public gun fight on a Springfield street corner in 1875. Hickok had won a watch in a poker game in a nearby saloon. The other man disputed the manner in which the prize had been taken from him. Hickok dropped him, with one shot from a revolver, dead at a reputed distance of 75 feet.

During the US Civil War (1861-1865), Missouri was disputed territory. While the state was officially declared to be part of the Union, the standing governor was an unabashed Southern sympathizer and tried to turn Missouri over to the Confederacy. The small towns of southern Missouri changed hands between the two sides so often that soldiers slipping back for a visit, whether they wore Union blue or Confederate gray, had to check carefully before showing up at home for fear of ending up a prisoner of war for the opposing side! Before, during and even after the Civil War, raiding parties who traveled under the guise of North or South were truly little more than traveling bands of thieves. Many used the troubled times as an excuse to rob and pillage isolated farms. From Jesse and Frank James and their contemporaries in the mid-1800's to the early twentieth century's Bonnie and Clyde and John Dillinger, they crisscrossed the Ozarks in their lawless travels. Many were later portrayed by Hollywood as misunderstood folk heroes, rather than the ruthless outlaws they actually were.

During the first half of the twentieth century, the Ozarks became notorious for moonshine and during the second half, for marijuana growth. At more than one point, marijuana threatened to become both Missouri's and Arkansas' #1 cash crop.

It was an incredibly strong pioneering spirit that spurred the majority of those who first came to this part of the country. They had to struggle against everything from the native people who lived here before them, to the natural elements. They even had to overcome such basics as incredible loneliness, in their quest to carve a life out of the wilderness known as the Ozarks. And yet, simultaneously the area seemed to attract a small but infamous minority population, whose primary quest was to get what they wanted, any way they wanted, and that included breaking the laws

Destruction

of the land. What was it that made the difference between these two groups? Was it the addition of outside chemical substances, from alcohol to marijuana to methamphetamine, that changed that personal drive to achieve into something else? We will probably never know the answer. What we do know is that the first was willing to invest in hard work with a never-say-die spirit. The second, on the other hand, seems to be driven by the more malevolent desires of their own heart, to have everything they want with much less effort.

Regardless, with an eye to its somewhat checkered past, it should not be such a surprise to law enforcement and others that the Ozarks has become the Mecca for meth production. Yet, we all remain surprised. Perhaps it is simply due to the fact that we want to believe our local culture had grown up and progressed past such pursuits. That, however, is painfully not the case, and both those coming from other parts of the country as well as those who have lived here their entire lives, can shed light on the violence and disaster that are the culmination of any journey down the road marked, Ozark Meth.

I shot out the windshield, a back window of a car, and a windshield behind me. I think it was a cop, and they were chasing us... somebody else was driving. I shot out the back window of our car, and their windshield, it caused their car to wreck, and we got away... the gun, a .45 automatic... we got away and we took the car up the mountains and hid it and I guess they burned it later on... we were carrying quite a bit of chemicals from Fresno to Sacramento [I skipped bond in Arkansas and ran to California and got caught later and extradited back to Arkansas for charges pending there]... —Danita

I'd get on a plane here at Springfield airport with a suitcase, I'd fly pharmaceuticals back and cocaine [before 9/11]... we got in a gun fight up there [Dallas] a couple of times, like territorial... we ran down the back stairs and there's a chain link fence with barbed wire and I got my pants tangled up in the barbed wire and I'm hanging upside down and I could hear bullets going by my head and I was shooting between my legs, upside down and finally, my pants ripped and I fell...
—Mark

What's the worst place in the country for drugs? I'd say Missouri, Springfield, but everywhere, I got 'em everywhere I went but it was easier in Springfield, to get about everything, anything... —Lynn

I pulled a gun on someone before because I thought they were wired and I was ready to shoot them if they were, but it was actually just a necklace... —Traci

We were going over to a friend's house because her roommate had beat her up and we were going there to start stuff with them... they opened up on us with a 9 millimeter and a shotgun... they were all my friends, my friends were shooting at me... we were all high and fighting and seeing things that weren't really there, and reading too much into things because the drug changes your whole way of thinking. You don't think like rational people do... —Taryn

It was constant, the major brawls... he'd trap me in a corner, and I cracked him with a rock and then he took the rock and hit me. He chased me down in a field one time. He told me he was going to kill me one time and I jumped out of the car in the middle of Springfield and ran down the road... every time I was high, he was high, that's why we had problems... —Julie

Destruction

We ended up putting each other in the hospital. He tried to kill me, I stabbed him 7 times. He went to jail and I remained homeless in Texas, lived on the streets for 10 days, but those 10 days to me, were an eternity... I then hooked up with a guy on the Internet, didn't even know him, I went there and he was actually transporting methamphetamines out of his shed. I thought he had a trucking company... he thought I knew too much and was going to kill me. I called my mother and told her I was going to die. She called my brother and he called law enforcement... I came out with a gun in my hand, higher than a kite, and I remember putting down the gun... —Mary Ann

I totaled 7 cars in 6 years, and the last time was so bad, I cut my nose and top lip off, and I had to have 156 stitches... [I also] went to the house to see the kids and of course, I was high, and they wouldn't let me in so I took a concrete turtle and I broke through a glass sliding door and they held me down and the police came and took me away. When I got to jail, I had to do a urine analysis and of course, it was positive for methamphetamine... —Miranda

I blew up a house one time, because I got real paranoid. Actually on the scanner, I heard the cops, I thought. I could have sworn I heard 'em say my address where I was, that they were coming and I turned a propane tank on, threw a lit torch in the door, as I was running out of the house. Blew up the whole house and the dogs died in there in the fire... —Danita

I used to fight with SE a lot and I would close my fists and I would hit him. Of course, he would hit me back and I'd be worse off than he was, but I had my nose broken twice. And even if I wasn't the one who initially acted violent, you're just in violence. It's just a violent situation. You live in a spirit of violence... he got into the vault business where he set up concrete vaults for

funeral services and so every once in awhile, he'd bring a vault home and we would, with all his friends, find a place and bury the vault and there'd be a lot of stuff we'd bury... illegal weapons, pills [for making meth], marijuana. He had a big thing about burying stuff...
—Miranda

He comes out and he's got guns in both hands and he's raising hell... he's crying because he's whacked out of his brain. He doesn't even know what's going on... I grabbed my girlfriend, we went and hid [running toward] her grandparents' house... her granddad comes out with his gun and his cowboy hat and cowboy boots... he asks us if we're all right... then they ended up having a shootout that lasted like 30 minutes... we hid in the culvert under the road and... we saw her grandfather walk in front of the opening of the culvert, fall to his knees and fall over... we thought he was dead... after he shot the grandfather, he went back inside the house, put down his guns, and cried to his wife... then the cops came, and took the grandfather to the hospital... and when I look back at all this stuff, I'm sitting here thinking, why in the hell did I stick around doing this stuff? Why? ... —Justin

That is the question that many friends and relatives ask...why? The answer on one level is provided by another of our respondents as she stated above, "Because the drug changes your whole way of thinking. You don't think like rational people do."

There is, however, another explanation as outlined by Steve Box, also a former meth addict, in his book, *Meth = Sorcery*, in which he offers the following: "Sorcery usually demands no special personal attributes and is practiced by anyone who can acquire the necessary magical substances. Sorcery is the work of ordinary persons using deliberate techniques and external means familiar to other adult members of this com-

Destruction

munity. The above describes how meth is made by people in the community, adult members showing others how to make it and whoever can get the necessary chemicals for its production. Sorcery is destructive magic that is regarded as anti-social and illicit. Illicit means not allowed or unlawful. This describes meth in our society.

Sorcery and witchcraft have five recurring elements: Performance of Ritual, use of material substances, objects that have symbolic significance, utterance of a closely prescribed spell, and prescribed condition of the performer. In the production of meth are these recurring elements:

1. Performance of Ritual. This encompasses the entire meth production process.

2. Use of material substances. These are the chemicals and ingredients used to produce meth.

3. Objects that have symbolic significance—beakers, thermometers, magnetic stirrers, stoppers, tubing, and flasks.

4. Utterance of a closely prescribed spell—the different recipes.

5. A prescribed condition of the performer or cook. This speaks for itself when cooking meth. The person is consumed by thoughts of power over others. Thoughts of, I'll never have to work again.

Another detail of witchcraft and sorcery is operating at night. When on meth, you sometimes don't sleep for weeks. Another detail of sorcery of meth is the fear of attack from the sorcerer on the people he supplies, but likewise the sorcerer can feel the same from certain people he supplies. Another detail is the closeness that meth engenders among participants using the drug together. It may satisfy a need for comradeship that is one of man's basic desires, but this can change to fear and paranoia almost immediately when on meth... Remember also that sorcery is also the ability to influence humans or natural events through supernatural power. This supernatural power is actually controlled by demons, devils, and Satan himself... the sorceries are blinding the truth. The truth about methamphetamine is that it is the purest form of sorcery on earth today. The biggest most subtle lie of Satan today is that meth is just another drug..."   Steve Box in *Meth = Sorcery*

Steve Box's book has become popular amongst meth users as they struggle to make sense of how they have reached a particular point in their journey. Former addicts affirm so much of what he writes, and this is true for many of those who spoke with us.

Meth is the devil, as far as I'm concerned. It's the devil in a powder form... —Karissa

The devil was in control of my life... —Lynn

Meth is the devil's drug. I don't care what anybody says. It is awful. It is the devil base. You love the evil side of life, the bad, the wrong, everything bad in life, you like. That becomes everything to you... —Meredith

There were shadows, darkness, whenever I was up too long. There was a lot of shouting at me, words that I heard in my head... phrases [like] I hate you. You're the scum of the earth... it's a feeling, a heaviness. It's a sense that there are no boundaries. There is no protection. There is no limits to negative influence [going on around you]... —Pam

Destruction

I usually stayed up until I collapsed. I handled it pretty bad. I remember I seen demons raping my little daughter once. I had a demon knock me off my feet in my own house. I was throwing rocks, real rocks, at my window. People don't believe these stories, or maybe they do. It's irrelevant. I'm telling you, when you step off into the demonic world, and you do meth, these things will happen to you... —Russell

[Meth] it's definitely the devil's tool... I was sitting on the steps in the garage and I saw the reflection in my mom's car window and I turned around and there was nothing behind me and turned back around and I saw his face and it was getting closer to me, like it looked like it was coming up behind me, but when I turned around it wasn't there... [He] had eyes of coal, pure evil. His face was pitch black and the eyes were just like the darkness of coal, but glowing still, it was just pure evil. I just knew... —Taryn

I was sitting outside a friend's house that I knew from high school... and the whole house was just kinda dark around it... like almost draped in black and on the porch, it seemed like 3 or 4 different demon-like shapes, and me and her could both see them. And we were freaking out and we sat there, watching these creature things, walking back and forth across the porch and then they disappeared and we didn't see them anymore... I went in and then she came to the door because she was scared because she said she could see them at a different house across the street... it was just devilish-like men... —Julie

Real, heavy demonic... when you're on meth, it's a hallucinogen. I believe it's connected of the spiritual realm. I believe that meth is witchcraft, because when I was on meth, when I was up for several weeks, I would see things. It brought fear to me. I would see shadows. I would see images, which you could call it a ghost or what have you. My partner and me, we used to see little green people... they weren't very tall. I didn't really see eye to eye, but they were just, chubby, real scary, you know. I know I felt a lot of fear when I seen them I don't want to say I was a tough guy but when that brought them, it really got my attention... every night, I would have physical demonic dreams... there would be so much pressure, like somebody had their whole body laying on you, and I'd be falling, and I remember just being so terrified in the middle of the night, and it was almost like I was fighting it physically, but spiritually together... I would try to scream something like Help! ... but it was like something would shut my mouth and I was just falling... —Moses

Yet, despite their fear as a result of these experiences, all of them admitted that these experiences alone were not enough to dissuade them from methamphetamine use.

At this time, I was living with my parents and they'd been saved. I would tell them about it [the dreams] but the thing about it was, they would pray for me, but I wasn't willing to stop doing my drug, and they wasn't able to relieve me, because my will was still saying, I'm doing drugs... —Moses

I think there is a general consensus, that [meth] is a demon; people need to know that it's a spiritual battle; it's a battle for your soul... —Michael

And so for many of those we spoke with, the journey that began as such a lark, the one they call party time, is now down to a grim existence, a nightmare. Unlike those in a dream gone bad, like Dorothy of Oz, waltzing along the yellow brick road or Alice in Wonderland falling down the white rabbit's hole, meth users cannot be roused back to reality with a gentle shake. The dreamers can simply sit up, shake their head and

Destruction

normal life returns. The meth addict's nightmarish life, however, has taken a turn from which they cannot just wake up. And all of its terrors continue and worsen, day and night.

Yet, despite all the problems caused by their drug habit and the life it has led them to, several of those who were former meth cooks, talked about their particular method of cooking and the product they made, with more than a bit of perverse pride. That ability to produce a prized variation of this concoction adds one more layer to the many reasons why those trapped in the meth culture, feel they cannot escape.

The recipe is so simple. It's easier than baking a cake... I actually saw him do it one time and by the third time [of me doing it] I'd improved the recipe... Actually people bragged, they told me I created the best. I believe it's sorcery. I believe who you are comes out in the dope. And I think, that's why, a lot of people sometimes they can make good dope and sometimes they can't. Mine was high quality every batch. My worst batch was better than most people's good batch... and I didn't skimp on product. I bought all new and I always had everything there and ready to do it... the reason it's sorcery, everybody has their own ritual, so to speak of doing it. Well, I had my own way and they tried to duplicate it, but they couldn't, even though they went through the same steps. Very rarely would theirs be as good as mine... —Richard

We owned 3 or 4 businesses, appliance repair, gas specialties, like Freon, anhydrous, all these things for torches... then my husband told me that we hired this technician and he called us over to his house one night and he showed us how to make meth. I said well, that would be good so we don't get arrested for selling and buying... we would stick that turkey fryer in the fireplace and get the Bunsen burner going and we'd just throw it in there with the batteries and the anhydrous and there's no smell... That process was real quick... I could make a batch in 12 minutes... my husband and I wanted it to be if you were standing over there, you wouldn't know what we were doing. And there were times where that would happen... —Jean

I didn't cook large batches. I just cooked small batches... you could cook it in a wine bottle and finish it within 24 hours and that was ideal for me... I've never met too many female cooks, you know. I've met a lot of females that their husbands were cooks or their boyfriends, or the guys they lived with, but as far as female cooks, I've never met too many... there's a real demonic force with meth. It's ritualistic...and people put you on a pedestal, people worship you because you know, the same people wanted everything [but] they would tolerate anything from me. I could behave and be and talk to them and treat them, just like any way I wanted. Walk in their house as if it was mine and just pick up things... I treated people in ways that I'm real ashamed of [now]... —Danita

And yet many continue to follow the road to its bitter end, where they suddenly come to a new realization, that there is nothing left for them.

While using, did you contemplate or attempt suicide?

I never attempted, but you think about it though, 'cause you get so depressed. You get bummed out. You always think who's gonna clean up that mess, and I just didn't want to make a mess... —Russ

Oh yeah. I tried overdosing on Vicodan. I thought the meth was going to kill me the last couple of times I did it. I thought I did too much. Even though I knew it was going to be too much for me, I still injected myself and

Destruction

took it, you know, even though I thought I was going to die... I've tried wrapping ropes around my neck actually... —Shanda

Yes, with a gun. My children walked in and seen me... —Lynn

I tried to commit suicide numerous times. Once I took 200 Xanex, another time was with meth, just meth and pills... I was tired, I finally got tired... —Lisa

I wanted to go out with a bang and so I would try to overdose. I didn't want to make a mess... —Deanna

Never really attempted it but I contemplated it a lot of times. A cry for help... —Russell

Consciously, never. Unconsciously, I think I was trying to kill myself every time I did dope... —Karissa

One time I decided I was going to wreck my car, and I was going around a big turn and I decided to just let my car go straight, my car turned anyway. I just let go of the wheel and it just followed the road... I just believe that was God's angels. He just reached out and took control... —Taryn

I contemplated suicide. It's methamphetamine and drugs, it's depression. When you start doing it, the reason that you're doing it, is because you think you don't fit in and once you start, you lower your self-esteem. Your whole life begins to drop rapidly. It just takes you down. It's just a bondage the devil has on you to take your whole life over and you go further and further... I tried to overdose. I've stuck shotguns in my mouth. I put guns to my head... I shot up a gram at once; the syringe was so full... I had to have somebody help me, and I remember when he stuck it in my arm, I just said, go ahead and put it in, and... he was just staring at me and he was saying, do you want to go? I just said, give it all to me... I was tired. I was tired of living that life... —Moses

And even without a suicide attempt, many find that after having lost so much, they know they cannot continue on this journey of destruction.

My children, my family didn't know I existed at one point, for a year. I thought I had no life. I just wanted to die... I had no home. I was shacking up once again, with another man, and all he wanted to do was to be high... and I had no place to go. My friend, I called him and he said get a bus ticket up here... and I never used again... 16 months ago... —Mary Ann

At that point, I had lost basically everything, from meth. I had lost my kids. I lost my whole family. I lost my house. I didn't have a job. I lost everything. I was at the bottom of the pit. ...I would walk around like a zombie... and that's when I figured, finally, I got to do something and that was it. Cold turkey... from that time, I found Jesus a week later... —Moses

I was sitting in the garage at like 2 in the morning, smoking a cigarette, and God had really been working on me, telling me, you need to stop this. You're going to die. I knew if I died I would go to hell 'cause I wasn't even trying to serve God and I saw a demon. I will never, ever forget it. I called my mom and told her, Mom, you gotta come over here and get me. I'm too scared to move...I just couldn't move and she came and got me back inside and I told her [I would go to rehab]... —Taryn

It's just all the emotional factors combined... if it's going to cost me my kids and everything else... when you lose your kids, that's pretty detrimental... —Russ

Destruction

For some, however, the end of the journey comes at an even greater cost, their health, their sanity, their very life. It takes the threat of losing something that vital to break the incredibly strong hold methamphetamine has on people's lives.

I used drugs until I literally have burnt out all my veins. In fact, I've been in the hospital a couple of times, and had different doctors tell me if I'm ever in a real serious accident, I better hope I'm unconscious because there's no veins they can reach easily, to give me blood or IV's ...I shot some dope in my foot and I missed it and it turned into a real big sore and it wouldn't heal. A couple days later I had like a 104 temperature, and my dope dealer just literally picked me up and carried me into the Emergency Room. They put an IV into me. They had to put it through my chest because I didn't have no veins to run antibiotics through me, [while they decided] whether or not, they were gonna take my foot off... I spent the time, sitting there on the phone, trying to find somebody to bring me a shot of dope, because I had a vein. The IV was in a vein... She got to the door of the hospital room and she said, oh no, you're crazy and turned around and walked away. And I cussed her and screamed at her... I didn't care whether or not they were gonna take my foot off, I was glad I had a vein, and I wanted somebody to bring me some dope... —Danita

My last relapse, I was gone for two weeks, and didn't even know where I was at. They said I had been in jail for 2 weeks, in the hospital part, just going completely crazy, beating my hands on the walls, and I was just totally out of it. They was at the point of sending me to a mental hospital, and what I do remember at the jail, there was a thin steel wall, and I would just keep beating my hands up on there, and hollering out to God, to Jesus, to save me... —Mike

I knew I was going to die and I knew that the people around me, just watching them use and watching their lives fall apart... horrible things happened... SE tried to commit suicide. He took like 300 pills, most of them were Xanexes. He was trying to kill himself and I knew a guy that shot himself... my next door neighbor, Dee came over one night. She was crying, and I tried to comfort her. Then they peeled out of the driveway and just about a mile down the road, she fell out of the car and died. We ran over her and she died. After she died, there was no more joy in it for me. It was just total pain. I wanted out after Dee died... And then SE came to get me to cook, and I couldn't go with him because I was too sick. I couldn't get out of bed. I was throwing up blood... I knew I was dying. And he left without me, and later that night, they called me and said that the police had arrested him and he tried to fight them off and his heart exploded and he died... he'd been using since he was 16 and he was 44 at that point... After SE died, I went and bought quite a bit of meth and I put myself in a motel room, and I was going to OD. And I didn't die. So about 3 o'clock in the morning, when I was still alive and still sitting there, I called my dad and I said, I don't want to die a drug addict. He said, "I can't help you but I can direct you to someone who can"... —Miranda

For many, the journey ends right here, either by virtue of their own decision or their own body or their sanity. They are finished with methamphetamine, and they have chosen to leave that world behind.

How many times did you try to get off and fail?

101. I had counselors that told me I was gonna lose my mind to schizophrenia if I used again and I believed it... —Pam

Probably at least 20, the last two years... —Miranda

Destruction

I don't think there's a number big enough... —Mike

Too many times to count... —Debra

20, 30 times... —Russell

I can't count that number. Too many... —Deanna

Lots. I can't even count the times. Over and over and over again... —Karissa

I can't count 'em. Tons. Tons of times... —Taryn

If I was gonna be just bone honest about it, I don't think I ever really tried to get off until I finally decided I was just sick of it... —Danita

For others, however, it is not that simple. For whatever reason, they do not make the decision to step out of the meth world on their own. Even if they, like many of their counterparts, have reached a point where they know something must change, they wait for someone else to make that decision for them.

[Cooking] just changed the whole level of usage, we had unlimited usage... I think there's a different spirit in it now than there used to be. There's something you know... I just felt more of an evil from it than before... I mean, I'm aware of it, but my husband always kept it away from me. He wouldn't let me get involved in any of it... I was just a user and a co-dependent... —Tina

At that point, I knew something was going to happen, I could feel it... bad, as in he's gonna kill me or the cops are going to come, we're gonna get busted. I get feelings and I knew things were getting ready to come to a stop... I remember laying on the couch, going Please God, something... God, just do something because I'm not strong enough to do it myself... and when I got busted, it was like, I didn't really mean that! —Debra

Leaving the Meth Culture the Hard Way

One of our respondents left the world of methamphetamine as the result of an explosion in his home, which happened as he was working with some of the chemicals involved in the cooking of methamphetamine. While he did not choose to exit his life in meth in this way, he came very close to exiting his earthly life altogether.

I can tell you what I was told, because I honestly don't [remember], my brain just stopped... it wasn't an actual cook. I was taking a lye bed, and trying to pull some more meth out of it... it was some fluids that were left over from several other cooks... after you collect so much, you just get rid of it, so you don't have no evidence... She [my wife] said that she heard a crack and I said, oh s—-, and then she said I was just in full flames... It was on a hot plate, and I guess it cracked, I don't know if it exploded. She just said there was fire all around me, and on me. She kept putting me out and I kept catching back on fire... We had a fire extinguisher and it didn't do nothing. I guess she got me in the shower. She said I walked back in there and I caught back on fire again. The last time I was running down the hallway with my head on fire, and I went outside. She put a hose on me, said I was like a candle, with my skin dripping down the side. I had second degree burns on my face and third degree burns on the rest, so yeah, I was lucky... I was in the hospital for three months and in the nursing home for two months, and [before that] in a coma for 7 weeks... and [when I woke up, they asked me] do you know why you're here? And I go, well, I don't know where I'm at. They told me. I asked about my wife and they said she was in jail, and then there was another blur for probably

Destruction

another week or two. So I had to go take those tank, scrub baths you know... they had me so doped up, I don't remember much, but I remember when I first woke up, I remember that.

As soon as I woke up, and I heard that it was methamphetamine, I mean, from that minute, from that very minute, I knew I was going to do something about it, all I can... I knew I had to do something, I just couldn't believe it. Six or seven weeks of your life, and not being able to remember... not knowing it and just someone telling you that. That's devastating... —Mark

Chapter 5

Intervention

In the United States, possibly more than in any other country in the world, such tremendous value is placed on individual freedom—the right to live in whatever manner we so choose—that it becomes exceedingly difficult to intervene in another adult's life. Intervention is difficult, even when it is painfully obvious that the decisions being made by an adult are leading to financial ruin and the devastation of a person's health and sanity.

By educating all involved, intervention is seen as a positive. There are people involved who care about the drug afflicted culture. Those addicted don't know they are cared about or how to be cared about. Being significant and wanting to be loved is the heart cry of each and every person alive. Intervention is a way to 'tell' someone they're cared for... I truly thought the stuff going through my mind was because I was a worthless person and I wasn't aware it was the drugs killing me... —Deanna

Intervention literally means to intervene, to step into, to invade someone else's life, when it comes to ways to short cut the methamphetamine journey. The first question that needs to be asked is a practical one. Is it even possible to pull a person out of the drug culture, to cut short their destructive journey and help them into recovery? Parents often do not even stop to ask the question. For those not paralyzed by denial or the ones who have moved past that step, they often assume that as the parent, they can and should step in. Of course, if their child is 17 or older, they quickly find there is little or no help available from law enforcement, despite their concerns for their son or daughter's health and safety. If the person is older, a spouse, a brother or sister, or some other relative, the risks and complications only intensify.

On no other question, are our respondents more perfectly divided than on the question of the timing of an appropriate intervention.

Would a well-timed and properly executed intervention program have brought you into recovery sooner?

Yes, definitely. Me and my wife, we worked together, if we would have had any idea of a support group where we could stay out of the public view, or help that we could get anonymously, but it seemed like at the time, anything we went to do would put [us] on the front page, basically, and everybody would know you were in a drug rehab... if we would have had any intervention that would have kept us out of the public view, then we would have taken it... —Jimmy

And despite the variety of drug rehabilitation programs currently available, many who have been all the way down the road have little faith in the ability of those programs to stop an addict who is not ready to give up their destructive behaviors.

Would a well-timed and properly executed intervention program have brought you into recovery sooner?

No, I do not believe so. I wasn't ready. You cannot receive help, like it's meant to be for you, until you're

ready. Every time before in my life, even if I thought I was ready, there was always that thought in the back of my mind that I wanted to go get high. That thought is gone now, and I don't have that thought anymore, and I know I'm ready, but before, no... —Meredith

Me personally, it wouldn't have, because I was full of pride. I was a so-called tough guy and nobody could tell me. If people told me what to do, I told them basically to shut up, or I don't want to hear it, or I would just walk away... —Moses

Yes, if I would have allowed it, and opened my mind and my heart and accepted outside help. I had to be ready myself, and be sick and tired of being sick and tired, like they say... one of my friends told me, you need help, and I called her a not-so-nice name, because I thought she was jealous, because here I have this glamorous life, which was no glamour whatsoever. Being homeless isn't glamorous, but that was the falsification and insanity of usage... —Mary Ann

Would it have helped me, back when I was using, before I went to prison? No, I don't know, maybe but... my dad was a police officer and I wouldn't listen to him. And if I wouldn't listen to my own family telling me, then, what makes me think I was going to listen to anybody else? I can't speak for other people. Maybe there are some people who can get it before they get in trouble, but I haven't seen that or hung out with very many people that have been there. They've always ended up in trouble before they've gotten off... —Lisa

I really don't think so. When I think of why I didn't see the red flags that were going up, it was because I didn't want to see them. I chose ignorance to be blissful and if you don't see it, you don't recognize it and you don't have a problem. The problem with that is you're not living in reality... I saw people depleting themselves. I *saw them basically killing themselves, left and right and yet, I still did it. That was something that I just overlooked because, well, you call this a culture, that was where I wanted to be at that time, in that drug culture...* —Justin

I don't think so. It's taken a lot for me to realize I need to quit. It took me losing everything including my freedom. Back then, I didn't have a house and I was too young to have a car so I really didn't have too much they could take away from me, so I'd say, no... —Traci

Yes, at the peak, when I was seeing my life being destroyed. At that time, but not before. There was nothing that anyone could have said or could have told me... —Michael

No, because I wasn't going to stop until I wanted to stop. And that's how it is with everybody. That's the one thing we all have in common. We're not going to stop until we want to stop. You have to hit rock bottom before you can... there's very few who get clean before they hit rock bottom. The lucky ones. I wish I would have been that lucky, but it took me hitting rock bottom before I [could stop]... —Karissa

And if many former addicts themselves are so adamant that even a well-timed, properly executed intervention would not have helped, then the question arises, how can we continue to search for and work towards more effective intervention techniques? Like so many other aspects of human behavior, there are no simple answers.

Intervention is the interruption of the destructive behavior that leads to an opportunity for treatment and ultimately, recovery. While the type and level of intervention varies, the keys are that the intervention(s) be consistent, concise, and continuous.

Intervention

"Intervention is what gets people to change their behavior," according to Charlie Maquire, a southwest Missouri Certified Substance Abuse Counselor with 20 years experience in this field. During those years, he has seen and worked with thousands of clients, with varying degrees of addiction severity.

"Without intervention, the addict continues to engage in destructive behavior that gets progressively worse. In addition, every person around them—their spouse, their children, their parents, their siblings—also suffers. Are we to simply sit back and watch as their negative behavior and its destructive consequences gets worse and worse?"

Like many others, both former addicts and professionals in the treatment field, Maguire states that timing is essential. "Early intervention and late stage intervention are the two more difficult, but for different reasons. Early often does not work because the individual has not had enough bad experiences. He or she can continue to deny the existence of a serious problem. In late stage intervention, the damage may be too severe, and the person has often reached a point where they no longer care. They have literally given up, especially if health problems have reached a critical point.

"Around the middle stage is often the best time, because by then, there is no more denying that chemicals are negatively affecting all aspects of life. It brings them into the reality that the negative consequences are a direct result of their chemical use."

Maguire continued, "There are different ways to do this. One is the *Step Approach*, in that it literally gives the addict an opportunity to fail in his or her approach to the problem. For instance, we agree to try it, 'their way' whatever that may be, and when that doesn't work and they have exhausted all their avenues, then they agree to do it, My Way.

"Any intervention interrupts the cycle of addictive behavior. Even if a preliminary intervention does not work, it makes it easier for the next intervention to take place and to be successful.

"The key is to discover what's most important to each person, and when chemical dependency threatens the loss of that one thing—whether it's family, health, freedom (due to incarceration), self-respect—we have found the button, that makes it possible for true intervention to take place."

Would a well-timed and properly executed intervention program have brought you into recovery sooner?

It's a hard question. I want to say both yes and no, because until I got jerked up with this offer, with the threat of a life sentence and knowing that I was gonna spend the rest of my life in prison... [Before] I always thought it was just a game... I didn't ever really think that it would ever get that serious... —Danita

Probably. I thought I was getting away with it. I thought nobody knew about it. Had I known that more people knew and they'd tried to intervene on that, then I might have. I didn't think anybody cared. No one ever tried. No one told me not to do it... —Debra

When I realized I had a problem, secretly inside, I wanted somebody to make me stop. And say, please don't do this to yourself anymore. Do you see what you're doing? And I saw what I was doing, but I didn't know how NOT to anymore. I didn't have a clue. I was already over my head but I didn't know how not be to high everyday. Yes, I wanted intervention... one time, I

Intervention

told my mom I had a drug problem, and she goes, do you need help? Do you need to go to a drug rehab or what? And I laughed and I said, No, I'll be fine, but... inside my head, I was going, Make me go! Make me go! And I don't know if that would have been successful or not, but she didn't. She didn't want to believe that I had as bad a problem as what I did... —Deanna

And just as the professionals tell us, for many, intervention is all about timing. The individuals, who are most deeply involved, agree.

Would a well-timed and properly executed intervention program have brought you into recovery sooner?

Probably. When I was 27, right after my friend got murdered and after I lost my kids that would have been a great thing for me. Maybe even before then, when J. first went to prison, when I was all alone, and I was raising two kids and I was stressed out, yeah... when J. went to prison and just when my grandma got sick and I thought she was going to die, I could have used [help]... —Shanda

After the birth of my second son, I was struggling, trying to be a single mother. I have 2 kids. I am trying to work 2 jobs. It was very frustrating, and it was like people would offer me help, if I would totally do it their way, or if I couldn't do it that way, the help was denied. I don't know what the right kind of help would have been, but that would have been the time, right then... —Miranda

Yeah, probably not at first, but with persistence. That's what it takes... we didn't get screwed up overnight, and we're not a trusting bunch, but if a man comes back and comes back and comes back, eventually something's gonna click... —Steve

And there lies another key, persistence and the belief that the person or organization offering the assistance really cares. But what does an intervention actually look like? It can take many forms, from the very simple to a highly organized team, ready to move at an appointed time. A conversation between one of the Intervention Ministry interviewers and Debra and her daughter, Karissa outlines a basic intervention technique that could be used by anyone, from a close relative to a concerned neighbor or church member.

As you think about this process, as a faith based group, we want to offer compassionate intervention. You didn't ask us to, but some of your friends did. That's the beginning of the process of intervention.

What could you tell us that would help us to convince people who need help?

You know, had somebody come to me, and said, hey, I know what you're doing, you need help, maybe I wouldn't have gone out and done what I did. At least it's a stepping stone in the right direction. I wish somebody would have come to me and said something like that, because maybe I wouldn't be where I'm at now...
—Debra

Did anybody ever go to you and say that?

Nobody like you. We did several times, for instance, the family, but nobody from the outside ever came in. There wasn't things like that years ago. Nobody spoke of it... —Karissa

What would you say to your mom?

I've got to tell them the story about the pamphlets. I just knew that she was sick, you know. When I was

Intervention

younger, I couldn't really put my finger on what was wrong, but I just knew she was sick. So I would get all these pamphlets from school, about drugs, and eating right, because she never ate... or she'd eat a lot. So I'd get these pamphlets and I'd put them around the house, and I'd fix her stuff to eat, and I'd always be crying, Mommy, it's good for you... —Karissa

That was your own attempt at intervention, trying to intervene in Mom's life, but Mom wasn't hearing it from you. What about someone like me, a neighbor and I know you. I know what's happening, and can see that you need help. What are we going to do? Would you have just said, you're out of your mind, back off?

Probably, because of the paranoia, but faith-based, and because you're my neighbor, that would kind of freak me out, because I'd be thinking, is she going to turn me in? Are they going to get child services on me? —Debra

If I'd come and said I have a place for you, where you can go, we'll put you up for a month and it won't cost you a dime. If I'd told you it's all faith-based and there are people there who will support you. What then?

[Right then] I'm not going to go for it, but if you leave your number, like on a card, and when I'm going through really hard times, I'm going to call you. It's gonna freak me out, 'cause you're there, but it'll give me something when I'm feeling bad... —Debra

What about follow-up calls?

Yeah, just call and say, I just wanted to call and say hey, I love you. Yeah, harassment in a loving way. Leave something behind, because we're not going to go for it at first, but when you're in need... I remember

laying there on the couch, just crying and praying... now if somebody had come and given me a card, I probably would have called. Maybe not right away, but I'd have eventually gone through with it, because it takes a certain point, before you're ready to accept any kind of help. You've really got to be on your lowest, most horrible day of your life... —Debra

Sounds like a pretty apt description of perfect timing, indeed.

In one sense, there may be as many different types and styles of intervention as there are individual addicts. Many are familiar with the family-style intervention as seen on various television programs.

My mom had taped this one show for me... and it was about a girl who had done meth and all of her family and her friends in her life all came together and they told her, she needed to get hold of [her life], or they were going to cut her off... They told her the things that they would help her with, if she went and got the help. She did go to treatment, and she left the state. I think for me, if people were to do an intervention for me, it would definitely have to be to throw me into some sort of ministry, because I've seen too many other people go to other rehabs, and myself having experienced other rehabs, it's just, they don't work... they would have to totally shut me off, away from the world... —Taryn

I'll tell you about the intervention I did receive. I was told by my sponsor, in a very, very confrontive way that I was in denial and what all that encompassed. And then I was also confronted by my friend, D., that I was gonna lose my daughter. And those two things were critical, and I was out of there within 3 days... —Pam

For many, however, intervention comes in the form of interdiction, literally, law enforcement enters the

Intervention

picture and the addict is arrested and sent to jail. Many times in the early stages, they are able to bond out and typically, many first-timers are placed on probation by the courts. For some, this first clash with law enforcement is enough to turn the tide and convince them that life must change.

I was lucky. I got arrested on the 11th and bonded out on the 13th... and as I left the courthouse that day, the message I got from my wife [who was still in jail] was that she hated me and never wanted to see me again and that destroyed me, that I had allowed it to go that far, to take the person I love the most, and that night was the lowest... I was in a motel room with my mother and she knew something was up and she handed me her phone and said, why don't you call your dad? So I called him... —Jimmy

I never wanted off until the time I was in jail. When I was in jail, I wished, I knew I needed to make some changes. I was arrested and it took 6 days to get bonded out... I totally underestimated [the damage it would do]. I didn't think I was hurting anybody but myself. I didn't realize until I was arrested, and seen the hurt in my parents' eyes, in my children, just how much, I totally underestimated... that was it. It scared me straight. I was one of those, once I started, I didn't want to stop and once I stopped, I didn't want to start. I'd be lying if I said I didn't want to do it right now, because I feel like I could do that and not get hooked again, but the consequences would be stupid...
—Duane

Going to jail, being incarcerated for 5½ months, I had time to just sit there and realize the right and the wrong in life, and everything. You have time and mental clarity happens after awhile, whenever you've been off drugs for awhile. And just all the guilt that comes, it just consumes you; with all the things I've done to hurt

my children and my family, so much. There's no way I can change that. There's no way I can ever fix that, but you know, you can't look back. You have to move forward, but that's hard and I don't want to live with anymore guilt like that. I have enough guilt built up from the things I've done to people that it's gonna last me a lifetime. I don't want to have anymore...
—Meredith

For others, that initial trip to jail did not make a serious enough impression to change their behavior. Others have to go to prison before they are ready to admit that the time for change has come.

I was arrested 12 times, all for methamphetamine... I'd get arrested, I'd go to jail, I'd get bonded out, I wouldn't quit. Then they'd get me again, and this process went on until the last few times... I'd make lawyers mad at me and I'd end up having to represent myself in court. They said me and my husband were a menace to society and a public nuisance and that we were very dangerous so they wouldn't let us out of jail, until we went to prison. That was the best thing they could have done for me... —Jean

In October I went to Missouri [from Arkansas] to do 120 days in a treatment program and it was real easy. 120 days is real easy to walk through. All I did was get real clean, told them what they wanted to hear, walked right through it. Got real clean, good and healthy. Got out in January and within a week I was cooking my first batch to pay off my lawyer... he was a $15,000 attorney. In a month and a half, I had him paid, all but just a couple hundred... I was arrested in April on a manufacturing charge... it wasn't pretty... —Danita

State mandated intervention, whether by means of an arrest, in which the addict stays in jail or goes to court-ordered treatment, has a dismal record, in terms of turning the addict permanently away from the destructive behavior that brought him or her to jail in the first place.

They made me go to stuff and you know, it don't do no good to go have a class with somebody and talk about bull crap. For me, the treatment did no good, because I had to go by force. We talked about things we did during the week and everybody lied, in my opinion, because everybody was there for the same thing. The parole officers made you go, the state made us go, and then you know, when you left there, people were joking, "Well, you wanna get high?" And I'd do the same thing. I'd be tweaked out when I'd go to the meetings...
—Richard

I went to three different rehabs... and I bailed out. I didn't want the authority and I didn't want the discipline... —Taryn

I've been to two other secular programs before and neither helped me. All they did was teach me about the drugs I was taking. They told me how many chemicals were in it [meth]. I was a cook. I already knew that. They didn't teach me how to stay off of it. They just taught me about it... —Traci

I went to Hannibal Council and I was there and I knew all the answers. You know, I was playing a game. I really wanted off, but yet I didn't want to look like I was such a bad addict, so I was playing along, writing everything they wanted to hear, and 13 days into my treatment, my counselor said, Man you are fooling us. She goes, you're not fooling me, you're fooling yourself. She said you can either get out, walk out, because someone else really needs your bed, or you can stay, and I'll start your 30 days over today. And I had this little nudge from behind me, and nobody was there, so I know it was God. I said I'll stay... —Mary Ann

In asking the individuals who have been on the meth journey, as to the best treatment options, the answers were as varied as the individuals themselves. A few basics did emerge, however, including the fact that the only secular programs known to have any success focused on overall behavior rather than just on substance abuse. That first wrong choice, choosing to use illicit drugs, may be connected to a maze of complex life issues. It may be impossible to ever sort out why that first wrong choice was made. It may be much more profitable to work on solving the problem at hand.

Were there specific treatments you found more successful than others?

I think the treatment centers themselves, each have their own individuality, however, I think it's the counselors and the way they communicate and approach residents in the center, because I had a powerful counselor and she was point blank. She took no crap from anybody, but she wasn't better than anyone else, either. She had been there, done that, you could tell it, without her even having to say it, but she had a compassion and was empathetic as well, and you could see that. She was really there for the residents. As a matter of fact, I called her last week and told her, I just wanted to say thank you, because you did make a difference in my life... —Mary Ann

The best one for me was getting arrested. Just by getting out of it. I mean, all of a sudden, I was off the farm. I couldn't tell my parents, I didn't feel like I could tell them, I needed to go to rehab. It's hard to explain. They're just old-fashioned and that was unacceptable...
—Duane

No, other than being incarcerated. That worked for me... —Meredith

Intervention

The rehab was good. Of course, prison is a real eye-opener. Living with 1,700 women is not fun. At least in prison, you got to go to school, go to work, you've got to, it's like its own little community... routine is good, whether you're there or whether you've on the outside. Routine is good... —Debra

I'd never been in treatment before, until I was in prison this last time. It was called the Gateway program and it was wonderful. [It's] behavior modification, more than it is drug treatment, but they work more on getting down to the root of everything and re-teaching you how to deal with those things, and how to deal with things going on in your life. They give you more tools than what a regular drug treatment program would do... —Karissa

I did 120 days in prison treatment, and I did a year in treatment in prison. It [helped] because it taught me self-esteem... they taught me a lot of things that I would have never stopped and learned if it wouldn't have been for them... —Lisa

For some it does not have to go so far. They can find help in simpler, less extreme ways

Abstinence is what it came down to when all was said and done. Treatment wise, it really came down to me sticking to my guns, saying, I am not going to do it. I'm not going to be that person. I don't want to be this. I don't want to be that, and sticking to it. Having the self-discipline to put it down and say no. Along the way, there were things that of course, stand in the way... but ultimately I feel like a better person when I accepted responsibility for sobriety, being clean and healthy... —Justin

I found that when you decide, and ... it was quite a long process for me, maybe the first time I started I got

it right, I had to quit hanging, ok? Change of playmates, change of playground, change your attitude... When you go to rehab, you gotta stay off the phone. I mean I seen hundreds of people on the phone when I was up there. Just like when you go to jail, you gotta realize, when you're in jail, this is your life. Your life's not on the street, so there's no reason to be on that telephone, wondering what she's doing or what he's doing, whatever. This is your life in here; you deal with it, same thing in rehab. You totally submit yourself to what you're doing... because the way I look at it, when I went there [rehab] I finally made a commitment to go there. No matter what they wanted me to do, I was willing to do it. And that's what it takes, a willing heart, because they are trying to rebuild your mind, rebuild your coping skills, everything... — Russell

If treatment is being around people that are doing the right thing, if that's a treatment, then that's what I did. I got around the CMA, Christian Motorcycle Association, and people like that... —Russ

There wasn't anything that I had to do, besides just decide that I didn't want to do it, and start going to church so I wasn't around the people that were doing it... —Lynn

I think I got a little bit of good out of all of it. My drug classes taught me a little bit about what the drug does to your body and your mind. That helped a little, but it wouldn't have done it by itself. My drug counselor helped me realize what some of the underlying issues were but that wouldn't have done it by itself. And coming to Christ and facing reality in a Christian way was the top of it, that was the main thing, but I think everything has its benefits... —Jimmy

And in bringing God into the equation, a whole new journey is opened up. The road now leads to a place marked, How To Get Off, but also How To Stay Off of alcohol and drugs, as told in the words of the people who know this journey better than anyone else.

Were there specific treatments you found more successful than others?

It would be Alcoholics Victorious. It started me out through everybody showing, you have to rely on God... I lived out by the St. Louis area at the release center, and I moved out here for a little bit, and I came out to the House of New Beginnings [in Bolivar] and it started me with a walk with faith in God... —Mike

I felt like I'd already gone to treatment before I went to treatment. My best treatment was finding God, although they had a spiritual element to Lafayette House treatment [where I went for treatment]... —Leilani

The first rehab that I went to, there was not even any mention of God in that, and it didn't work. After Teen Challenge, I've known that God has been with me, this whole time, because I should have died a long time ago... —Lynn

Alcoholics Victorious... we actually talk about Jesus... —Moses

God is a big answer to your drug problem. You lose all contact with God when you are there with drugs. God is the only way out, you just give your problems to God and work with Him, to work you through them and it's going to work. And that's the only thing I've found so far that works... —Meredith

And that leads to Deliverance which ultimately leads to Life!

How Were You Treated?

When asked specifically, our interviewees responded at a rate of nearly 3 to 1, that their treatment by law enforcement and the courts was fair or better than fair. A few felt, however they had been mistreated by individual officers or that the law enforcement system had failed them in some way.

Was the treatment given to you by law enforcement and the courts, fair?

The first time, no, because the officer hit me in the back of the leg because I wouldn't get down on my knees. The anhydrous had sprayed me and I was freezing cold... and 'cause I wouldn't bow down and get on my knees, he slapped me in the back of the legs with a black jack... —Richard

I hate to say this, we were not bad people, we were just doing drugs... they kicked the door down and missed our 5 year old daughter by just this much... they scared our kids to death. I didn't give them no struggle, no fight, no nothing. There was no guns. We had no history as violent people. They just terrified our kids. If they'd have done their research... —Mark

No, because they don't take into consideration, the things in my life that play the large part in what brings about why I do it, why I've done it, what drives me to do it... the anguish, all the hurt, the loss of everything. I went to prison at 16. The lack of my father and the lack of a family structure... —Lonnie

No, but it's kind of a tough statement, because at the times when I needed them to actually step and say, hold on a second, there's got to be something else here, they didn't. But whenever I'm getting pulled over every day, because I don't have tags on my car, and of

Intervention

course, that's their job and they're supposed to, but they didn't have to put me in jail every time... —Justin

Seventeen per cent of our respondents had not been arrested and had no personal experience with law enforcement. Of those, who had dealt with law enforcement or been through the entire system, including courts and prison, the overwhelming majority felt like they had been treated appropriately.

Was the treatment given to you by law enforcement and the courts, fair?

Yeah, I didn't think so at the time, but you never do, when you're first coming off of drugs. You think they're being mean, why are they picking on me, how dare them. I wasn't hurting nobody but myself, but in reality, you are hurting people. You might just be doing drugs yourself, but it affects your family and your friends, so yeah, they were fair... —Debra

Yes, they did... I never tried to find help. I knew when I was going to prison. It had got to that point in my life. I knew eventually I was going to be busted and when it happened, I was grateful because it saved my life. It really did... —Lisa

Oh yeah, for the most part. There are some guys who don't but that's just common. A lot of them [officers] believed in me. A lot of them liked me. There's a lot of good cops in Bolivar... —Russell

I'm sure I thought at the time, I was getting a raw deal. We gotta rationalize everything. I'm sure I was treated fairly. [It] was a pretty eye-opening experience. In fact, it probably saved my life at that time... —Steve

Yeah, I believe it was fair. I do believe they should have been harder on me. When I say fair, it was in my favor.

I felt like they were a little lenient on me, more lenient than they should have been. In looking back, I know I deserved worse, but some kids you can arrest them and then that's it. They straighten up, it scares them. Nothing was gonna scare me. I was in it for good...
—Miranda

Yes, they were very fair. They need to be harder, because I've been pulled over so many times with meth on me, you know, and they really never searched me. I mean they have a few times, and I would hide it really good on myself, and they'd search me, but they wouldn't find it. I think they need to go into detail searching a little better, you know... —Shanda

It was fair. I felt like I had a really bad attorney, but [the officers] treated me cordially. They treated me with respect, I thought... —Duane

Yes, but they should have been harder. My case is probably not like anybody else's—my brother's a judge. At that time, he was a prosecuting attorney. My lawyer was his friend from law school. I paid no restitution. I paid no lawyer's fees. I learned no lesson so I continued to do it... —Mary Ann

Yes, they were real good. I don't think they should have been harder or easier... when I was incarcerated for 5 months, I was there long enough to realize a lot of things that I want to do different now in life. They were really good. They were hard enough to where it took me awhile to realize the whole concept of jail—that it's not supposed to be enjoyable. These people aren't here because I've been good. They're here because I've done something wrong and bad and I need to suffer the consequences. They were strict enough that you learned how to walk a fine line to where you did what you're supposed to do. It kinda gave you structure, I guess, but yet not overbearing to the point where they were [doing

Intervention

the] cruel and unusual punishment type of thing. They did really well. I learned my lesson. They were awesome at that... —Meredith

Now that I'm saved and I got Jesus in my life, I think that I was treated real fairly... —Moses

Interview with Deputy John Young

John Young of the Laclede County Sheriff's Department has spent the last 3 years doing nothing... except fighting meth. Working in close cooperation with both state and Federal agencies, such as the Missouri State Highway Patrol, the Drug Enforcement Agency (DEA) and the US Attorney's Office, Deputy Young has been operating under a Federal grant through the local sheriff's office. His only job—fight meth in Laclede County. His only words for anyone considering trying methamphetamine, "Don't Start!"

Deputy Young states that the good news in the local battle against meth is that the number of clandestine meth labs found in this part of the state has dropped off markedly in the first half of 2005. That makes the fight against methamphetamine somewhat safer for local law enforcement officers who are not dealing with unknown chemical substances, when they make a drug bust.

The bad news is that meth is now being brought into the Ozarks in large quantities by the Mexican mafia which makes its product in large labs south of the border and cuts it with cocaine or opium or even other true pharmaceuticals like amphetamine. The reason is simple economics. Even locally made meth costs more to produce than the foreign made variety.

Compared to other drugs law enforcement has had to fight in the past, Deputy Young and others find meth much more overwhelming because of its addictive nature and the fight against the local meth labs. "You don't find people making heroin or cocaine in the trunk of their car," he stated. "The high is over in an hour with cocaine, for instance. You also don't find yourself dealing with someone who hasn't slept in days. Cocaine doesn't attack the brain the same way and do the same kind of damage that meth does. The medical community also has proven treatments for those drugs, not so, with meth."

Even so, John Young is living proof that the answer to methamphetamine is based on relational contact. "What we need, as do a lot of other communities, is a talk line, for people to call in and just talk, to get information or find out about treatment options People use me for that right now. Somebody calls, that I've arrested before, to say, 'I'm trying to go straight and this person won't leave me be, can you do something about that?' Other times, it's someone who is trying to stay off of drugs, but when a new crisis comes along, the wife/girlfriend leaves or there's a death in the family, they suddenly find themselves reaching out to use again. If they call me, or someone else to talk it out, rather than use, that's a good thing. A definite step in the right direction."

Deputy Young concluded, "In the past, communities have always made the drug user out to be a low income person, the poverty-stricken, the low life from the wrong side of town, but that is not the case anymore. With meth, everyone is involved."

Enabling and Co-dependence

Two common, yet difficult syndromes identified by family therapists, as enabling and co-dependence haunt many families who struggle with drug and alcohol addiction. Both make it easier for initial addiction to take root in a family and both make it easier for addictive behavior to continue and for the addict to blame others for his or her problems and unacceptable behavior. Remember, that many times, these unhealthy behaviors may have been going on for years, before an actual addiction is identified. They may also be seen in many families where addiction is not an issue.

Celebrate Recovery, a Christian-based 12-step program that brings addicts and their families together, to fight all forms of addiction, has defined both terms for all who need to understand how these behaviors support and encourage addiction.

Celebrate Recovery—ENABLING

Enabling is defined as reacting to a person in such a way to shield him or her from experiencing the full impact of the harmful consequences of behavior. Enabling behavior differs from helping in that it permits or allows the person to be irresponsible.

PROTECTION from natural consequences of behavior.

KEEPING SECRETS about behavior from others in order to keep the peace.

MAKING EXCUSES for the behavior (to school, friends, legal authorities, work, other family members).

BAILING OUT of trouble, such as paying debts, fixing tickets, paying lawyers, providing jobs or housing.

BLAMING OTHERS for dependent person's behavior (friends, teachers, employers, family, SELF).

SEEING THE PROBLEM AS THE RESULT OF SOMETHING ELSE, such as shyness, adolescence, loneliness, child, broken home.

AVOIDING the chemically dependent person in order to keep the peace (Out-of-sight, out-of-mind).

GIVING MONEY THAT IS UNDESERVED/UNEARNED.

ATTEMPTING TO CONTROL, by planning activities, choosing friends, getting jobs.

MAKING THREATS that have no follow-up or consistency.

TAKING CARE OF the chemically dependent person, especially by doing what he/she should be expected to do for themselves.

Celebrate Recovery—WHAT IS CO-DEPENDENCE?

My good feelings about who I am stem from being loved by you.

My good feelings about who I am stem from receiving approval from you.

Your struggle affects my serenity. My mental attention focuses on solving your problems or relieving your pain.

My mental attention is focused on pleasing you.

My self-esteem is bolstered by relieving your pain.

My own hobbies and interests are put aside. My time is spent sharing your interests and hobbies.

Your clothing and personal appearance are dictated by my desires as I feel you are a reflection of me.

Intervention

Your behavior is dictated by my desires as I feel you are a reflection of me.

I am not aware of how I feel. I am aware of how you feel.

I am not aware of what I want—I ask what you want. I am not aware—I assume.

The dreams I have for the future are linked to you.

My fear of rejection determines what I say or do.

My fear of your anger determines what I say or do.

I use giving as a way of feeling safe in our relationship.

My social circle diminishes as I involve myself with you.

I put my values aside in order to connect with you.

I value your opinion and way of doing things more than my own.

The quality of my life is in direct relation to the quality of yours.

Chapter 6

Deliverance

"But we see Jesus, who was made a little lower than the angels, now crowned with glory and honor because he suffered death, so that by the grace of God he might taste death for everyone. In bringing many sons and daughters to glory, it was fitting that God, for whom and through whom everything exists, should make the author of their salvation perfect through suffering... Since the children have flesh and blood, he too shared in their humanity so that by his death he might destroy him who holds the power of death—that is, the devil—and free those who all their lives were held in slavery by their fear of death... Because he himself suffered when he was tempted, he is able to help those who are being tempted."

—Hebrews 2:9-10; 14-15; 18

As we reach the end of the meth journey, it is appropriate that we cast a glance back, once more, at the diversity of these thirty people who have shared the stories of their lives on methamphetamine. They have come from different places, and many originally, are from other parts of the country and have come to make the Ozarks their home. They have different backgrounds, vocations, educational levels, and family dynamics and yet almost all have arrived at the same destination as they leave the world of methamphetamine behind.

One night I was sleeping, it was cold and I was on the top bunk. I was dreaming I was walking with Jesus... I kept looking and I asked, "Are you Jesus?" And he goes, "yes", and all I remember is his eyes hugged me. I saw his beard and people asked me [later], what did he look like? I said, I don't know... I just know his eyes hugged me. He had on a white robe... and we were walking and I realized my feet aren't even touching the ground. I'm up here with Jesus... He says, "why are you looking down?" I go, "I'm not looking down." He says, "I promise, you will not stumble". And boom, he was gone. I came crying out of that jail cell and there were all these women... and they said, you found jailhouse religion. I said, "You bet I did! You bet I did!"... —Jean

At that point, I had lost basically everything. From meth, I had lost my kids. I lost my whole family. I lost my house. I was at the bottom of the pit... I found Jesus a week later. I found Him and ever since then, when I fully found the Lord with all my heart, it was day and night. A night and day situation. One morning I woke up and my heart just decided to sing to the Lord. I know it was the grace of God. I know it was all of God... in the whole 9 years [of using], it was 3 or 4 times a year. I would quit for like a day or a week or something and then I would go right back to it. I just couldn't do it but OK, I just want this on the record, beyond a shadow of a doubt, it is the power of God that changes lives. I'll do the whole interview on Jesus and I give all glory and honor to God... —Moses

I just turned my life over to God. I was in prison and I was tired of the life. I knew I couldn't do it on my own. There was no way. I just surrendered to Him. Without Him, I couldn't make it... —Lisa

Not everyone in this group went to jail, and the same is true in the greater world, in terms of those who become addicted to methamphetamine. Not everyone goes to jail. Many end up in a prison of their own making, addicted to a substance that gives no quarter, creating a situation in which they can see no way out. Several had used meth for years but had never been arrested. Still, in their search for a way out of the world of methamphetamine, they came to a similar conclusion.

How did you eventually win the battle and get off of methamphetamine?

Jesus Christ. I have had no withdrawal from meth. I'm living with a Christian woman who has been my sponsor for the last year. I got out of my situation. I'm not around it. I'm not living with users anymore. I go to Alcoholics Victorious once or twice a week. I go to church on Wednesdays and Sundays. I'm hanging out with Christians. I'm talking to Christians every day on the phone. I haven't missed a meth rally. I'm just walking in the Spirit... without Jesus Christ; you don't have anything to fill that hole. There's got to be something to fill that hole once the drug is gone... somebody told me, in the last 3 or 4 months [of using] because I thought I had to be clean before I could go to the Bible or I could go to God. But they told me it was OK, and that was the meth support group... It's with a peace and it's with a clarity of thought. It's with a firm belief in the truth... I have learned to call Satan a liar and tell him to get behind me, and to claim the blood of Jesus Christ, because I've been in bondage, but God is victorious... I don't conceive of a set back. I believe that I've been delivered... —Pam

With Christ there was no withdrawal. I found nothing but Christ is successful... Every day I get up and I read the Scriptures and invite Christ into my life and [ask] him to guide my footsteps and keep my mind away from dope and just be a part of my life... —Richard

After SE died, I went and bought quite a bit of meth. I put myself in a motel room and I was going to try and OD. And I didn't die. So about 3 o'clock in the morning, when I was still alive and still sitting there, I called my dad and I said, I really don't want to die a drug addict. He said, I can't help you but I can direct you to someone who can. That meant that he knew I needed Jesus in my life... that first year I went to Teen Challenge in Michigan. I came home after a few weeks. I was a wreck and my parents sent me on a mission trip to Mexico, and when I got back from Mexico, I just began to start telling my story. I started talking about the little things I could, you know, I was a drug addict and God saved me. God set me free and it was like the more I would talk about it, the freer I would get, and I just kept talking... —Miranda

I was delivered. God delivered me. When I went to Teen Challenge in Michigan, the first time, they took me to church. I went to the altar and asked God, I need some help. I can't do this by myself. I don't want to be hurting the people I love. Please help me and I got saved that day. When I walked away from that altar, it was like I was a new person, 'cause I've not had any desire, NONE to do any drugs. I've seen a lot of people. I've seen the dope and I just feel sorry for them people. I really do. I have no desire to get high anymore...
—Lynn

I went to church and I got baptized and I just found so much support through God, and the people at church...
—Shanda

God totally delivered and restored me... I'd just felt God tugging on me for a long time, and I was beginning to weep, because I wanted to be right with God, and [the people at church] laid hands on me and I was delivered and I felt the deadness come out and God filled me up again spiritually. I was baptized in the Holy Ghost. I got refilled that night and started praying in tongues and I just knew, you know, that was it... I was in a rehab and it was a 90 day program but I left after 3 days. I know God brought me there, just to get my deliverance 'cause I got it... Before I went to that last rehab, when I tried doing it on my own, and I would get really sick, bloody vomit, bloody diarrhea. I couldn't move because I'd be that sick, without the drug. And then after I was delivered, [no more]... —Taryn

And even though some admit that it took them awhile to realize their only true hope was in Christ, once they made that decision, life took a definite turn for the better.

Through obedience to the Lord, through a drug rehab and through just sacrifice...just surrender your will. ...I go to counseling through my church and just being enlightened with the knowledge of the Bible... when it all comes down to, there was always one thing I turned to and that was God... —Russell

I moved away from that town, buried myself in the Scriptures, and started asking God to take control of my life, and help me beat that addiction. He did, and now I've got the strength to stay away from it... —Michael

I'm not the most religious person but when I was in jail... I didn't realize until day 5 in jail, as I was sitting there, feeling sorry for myself, thinking it doesn't get any worse than this, and then it hit me. God tried to give me warning about a year before, when I fell asleep at the wheel with 4 kids in my car. I don't remember too much of it, just that I woke up, and I know it scared them bad and it woke me up to the point where I said, I gotta make sure this never happens again. But my thinking was, I gotta make sure I never run out, which was wrong. I realize...he was giving me a warning and I didn't get it. In jail, it came back, that was my first warning. I didn't get it so it had to come down to this... I hadn't prayed in a long time... and I prayed that night and everything just started coming... and I knew God was telling me... —Duane

I'm quitting for me and the Lord... I remind myself if I use again, my addiction will be worse and I'd probably be dead or in prison or Lord knows where. I got my house back. I got a better vehicle now and God just keeps blessing me, whereas when I was on Satan's side, I was losing everything... —Traci

The fact that I am sitting here in the free world right now is an act of God, because I know my jacket [my record] and they had every right to give me that life sentence... —Danita

If meth is of the devil, which is certainly what a majority of these respondents stated in no uncertain terms, then it should come as no surprise that the best weapon to fight the plague of methamphetamine is none other than Jesus Christ. He is, according to those who know this battle better than anyone else, not only the one who delivers those addicted to meth, but He continues to be their source of strength on a daily basis as they live each day of a new life, free of the curse of meth.

Do you have help staying off? What are your relapse prevention techniques?

The Lord. Just knowing that I would be letting Him down completely by going back to the life that He helped save us from... just church and staying within our walk with the Lord... —Julie

He's the only thing... —Lisa

Deliverance

I can go and sit in my room and if I have the urge to do something, I have a little pow-wow with God and it'll just seem to ease off, slip away and it's getting better everyday, you know... —Steve

I got 2 main sources. One of them is the Word of God, and the other one is prayer. That's what helps me. The Word of God, the power of the Word is unbelievable. It's unreal. Jesus, He speaks to you daily. My pastor taught me this. That book isn't about somebody. That book IS somebody. And I know one thing for sure, if it wasn't for me reading the Bible, if it wasn't for me getting on my knees and praying and crying out to God and putting everything aside, I would not be here right now... —Moses

Anytime I have to go back to [my hometown, where I got addicted], I stop and pray before I go and I put on the armor of God. That's all I have... —Michael

The word of God. Prayer from everybody. My grandparents and my mom. If they hadn't been on their knees, I have no doubt in my mind, I'd be dead... I keep myself plugged into church and plugged into the Bible... —Taryn

My only source for help in staying off drugs, is serving God. My day starts when I wake up, I praise God for another day and through that day, I ask him to put people in my path that I can witness to, in some small form or another... because He's the only way to stay clean... —Jimmy

I'm ignorant at religion. I don't know it. I'm trying to learn and I'm understanding it but I can't talk it. I can't sing it, but I've been reading it and I have been studying and I have been watching a lot of things, 'cause I know there's a God, and I know that's why I lived... —Mark

In addition to their own prayer and Bible study, most find that support groups keep them going in the right direction, whether that group is a 12-step program or simply the people at their church.

I am very involved in Alcoholics Victorious. It's a faith-based Christian 12-step recovery, and there are just no other meetings for me to go to. I have a substantial number of people at church. I lead the youth group. Anytime I need to talk, I have a number to call, whether it be my mom, or another recovering addict...
—Mary Ann

My AA group was really centered on God, and that's what helped me. Seeing all these people from all walks of life, from megabucks to poor. And each one of them, told me something about myself and usually, when you saw somebody and you said, well, that guy don't have nothing to offer me, he's usually the guy who hit closest to home... —Steve

AV [Alcoholics Victorious] is my big support. My church helps me tremendously. I stay active in my church. I'm a leader with the youth... I just praise God that He's let me survive this long... —Mike

A relatively new response to the meth epidemic is the *Freedom From Meth Rally* and it is gaining force in southwest Missouri. There are several groups sponsoring the rallies, which usually consist of a Christian band that performs, on a Saturday afternoon or evening and is followed by speakers who are meth survivors, now in recovery. These are the people who know the meth battle most intimately and who personify hope when they literally hold out a hand, offering the opportunity to any in attendance, to step out of the meth life and embrace sobriety.

Meth rallies require substantial advance organization that includes the establishment of a weekly support system that is ready, willing and appropriately prepared to offer services to the meth addict who is attempting to walk away from his or her former life. In addition to salvation through Jesus Christ, meth rally supporters are ready to offer the addict a place to live, if necessary, treatment options and counseling opportunities that are accessible and realistic. Food is served. Books, T-shirts, bumper stickers, and a variety of other anti-drug resources are also available, touting Freedom From Meth, and a life based on something greater than drugs and the destruction they bring.

As a regular supporter, worker, and attender of the Meth Awareness Rallies, my life has been changed. I have become aware that I was blessed enough to be rescued 10 years ago. All our lives are affected by those we have conversations with. The mothers who cry. The teenagers who have no emotion on their faces because they were dragged there. [Then] there are the teens who have found a better way of life than drugs. The faces of those who come to the rally high, but are there because they want a better way of life. The rallies, meetings, jails, courtrooms are full of the faces of those who can't stop doing drugs, even at the expense of living in a cage for years. Those addicted are having their lives changed because someone cares enough to get involved—personally involved in their lives! As one who has been delivered from drug addiction, I can say that I might not have gone so far into addiction as I did, if I had been aware of the facts... I truly thought the stuff going through my mind was because I was a worthless person and I wasn't aware it was the drugs killing me...
—Deanna

All of the hype, advertisement and stuff that surround the rallies are enticing and impressive, but without a doubt, the heart of the *Freedom From Meth Rallies* are the volunteer efforts of the former addicts, who courageously stand before the crowd and share their stories. For their words only tell a part of the story. The rest of the story can be seen, as strong men and women, of different ages, backgrounds, and vocations, allow themselves to be used by God to help others. They also make up the backbone of the follow up effort, which is the support group, that continues to meet regularly, offering ongoing services to those in need, long after the rally folks have gone home, or moved on to the next rally site. That's not to say that they forget about the newly freed, for those folks are kept abreast of the next rally and the next, and encouraged to come, share in the excitement once again, and in a few months, perhaps even become one of the new rally presenters.

It is also not unusual to see addicts from one town choose to step out at a rally or attend a support group at a different community, some distance down the highway from their hometown. If that is what it takes to make them more comfortable and able to come to terms, especially in the beginning, with their addiction, so be it. The important part is taking that first step, wherever that may be. The support group, then, continues to meet on a weekly basis and offer a place of shelter, warmth, friendship, and advice, all based on the words of the Savior who instructed in John 13:34, "A new command, I give you: Love one another."

And that is exactly what methamphetamine survivors do. For reasons that are not yet completely understood, those serving in the war against meth, have found that survivors of the ravages of methamphetamine, are more driven than other recovering addicts, to reach out to their brothers and sisters who are still struggling.

I've taken the classes and I really enjoy telling [my story], if I can help a teenager, keep 'em from doing alcohol or drugs, this world will be a lot better off. I believe that is really what God wants me to do... to share my experiences with the younger youth, and show 'em... —Mike

... But I know now that I have a purpose in life, and it is to go out and help these people that are on drugs. Give them some hope, to help bless somebody else... —Lynn

I'm a full-time youth pastor... I made it a point [with] everybody I used to hang around, you want some help? You want Jesus? You can talk to me and I'll do whatever I can... my family has all moved out here from California, all my family. My sister is moving here soon and I've got one brother who is still incarcerated but all the rest are here... —Moses

The number one thing that's on my mind now more than anything is the meth problem. I get so mad at myself because it's just continuously running through my mind. I'm trying to think of ways to get money, to do things if there's a difference I can make, something I can say to kids... —Mark

I lead the youth group at my church and they ask me questions regarding my addiction, and I have no problem, telling them exactly about it. I brought my [teen] daughters to the meth rally. At first, they crossed their arms and balked but now they've invited their friends to go to the next one, because they've seen the excitement and how their mom is clean and sober today... —Mary Ann

I see myself working in a facility, totally devoting my time to women, who have been battered or are drug abusers, who need this deliverance and showing them, there is a way through Jesus Christ... —Taryn

I think what's gonna help people more than anything is seeing people like me, stay off meth and stay in church. Our prayers and our going by and saying, hey, we love you, we care and we're praying for them, and showing them that we care, even though they're still using...
—Richard

... [After I'd been off about 6 months] I met a lady and she said, "I've been praying. I don't know you, you don't know me but I feel like I'm supposed to give you this money". What it was, there was somebody who had gotten me into Teen Challenge in Michigan, he had a brother in Hong Kong who worked with heroin addicts, 42 years there as a missionary. And he said he would love to see me go work with his brother, with the heroin addicts and I thought, there's no way that'll happen. But this lady comes up to me out of nowhere and gives me this money and we buy a plane ticket and I go to Hong Kong. I lived in Hong Kong, China and the Philippines for 3 months, giving my testimony and traveling around working with heroin addicts, but it was as much rehab for me as it was experiencing their rehabilitation... —Miranda

And that is literally a major part of what it is all about. Unfathomable as it may seem, having survived what they have in terms of the ravages of meth, these same recovering addicts have found an exciting way to amplify their own salvation, in reaching out and helping others to claim a share of this new life, a life with all its rich promise, a life that is free of the addiction to methamphetamine.

In that same spirit, we asked them *the* biggest question with which our nation and our governments, national, state, and local, have been struggling for some time. There seems to be no consensus in the answers, not from government officials and not even from former

Deliverance

addicts, yet each gives us a part of what may eventually become the complete answer.

What is the best way to handle the methamphetamine problem?

Raise awareness, more education... —Mary Ann

Education from kindergarten on... we don't give kids enough credit for being as smart as they are... we need math, reading, drug education... no sugar- coating... I wish I had known more about meth before... —Leilani

More education... —Debra

I think they should teach the kids at a younger age, to where they know... I think 7 is a good age, because they really understand... —Shanda

Exactly what they're doing right now, taking the pseudoephedrine and putting it behind [the counter], where they can keep an eye on who buys all this... —Mike

Stop the production... —Deanna

There are thousands of people making it. It just seems like when one goes to jail, 3 more cooks pop up. I do know in the drug world, you've got your head cook and he will take 2 or 3 people under his wing, so if he ever goes down, there's 3 people he's taught how to make the drug, like he makes. These people are sworn to silence, otherwise you die, and he teaches them and then if he goes to jail, each of those 3 teaches someone else, and then it's kinda like a chain reaction... it's just like unstoppable... —Meredith

Bust 'em, send 'em to jail... —Lisa

Lock them up... —Justin

I think law enforcement ought to try helping people instead of imprisonment, because [that] just makes people rebellious. They come out harder from being in there... that's why the revolving door is happening in prison. If they took the steps to really help people, rather than imprison people, then there would be less drug use... the best way to handle the meth problem is getting recovery centers that are based on the foundation that Christ is the answer... —Richard

The Lord... —Julie

God is the only way... —Karissa

Ask God for deliverance... —Lynn

Get with Jesus. Lots of accountability... I strongly believe in my heart, that if there be a man full of passion of Jesus Christ, that wants to help and reach out to others, I believe that we could take over... put God in your life... —Moses

The best way for society to handle the methamphetamine problem is that we need to get our churches a lot more involved than they are... get our churches working with law enforcement, because from what I've seen most of our people who are on meth, are not necessarily convicted criminals or people who want a criminal life style, but they are stuck in a rut, and they don't know how to get out. They're in bondage, and the only thing that will set them free is the deliverance of Christ Jesus... if we can get our Christian people to understand more about methamphetamine and not be so condemning, then I think that's the key to helping this problem... —Jimmy

Deliverance

Prison is not the answer... it's going to have to be a deal where people who want help can get the help they need, treatment and to get their self-respect back... it's gonna have to be where they can get their health care, food stamps, whatever they need temporarily until they can get back on their feet... otherwise, they go right back to doing it again, because they've got to feed themselves. It would definitely be faith-based. It's kinda going to have to be a deal, the whole works, services to the whole family. I think everybody can change and I think everybody deserves a second chance... they would have to know coming in, that this is a one shot deal. You're giving your best effort... I wouldn't do it but one time [if they fail] I wouldn't let them back in the program, make them go to prison... —Mark

Show me that you understand and give me love. Let me know that there's help and there are people out there who understand completely... —Michael

You could take everything off the shelf [they use to make it] but I really think through prayer is the only thing I can see, because if you take everything away, they'll just come up with a new drug. I don't know how to fight it without God... —Traci

Well, I don't want to sound corny, but I believe Jesus Christ is the only way, because you can see a meth addict come in that is totally high and get saved and God can deliver them. Whereas they can go through every rehab, every program, and you can try to eliminate the products that they buy to make the meth, you can try to crack down here or crack down there, but until people are delivered, I mean, truly delivered, they're always gonna find a way to get their stuff. I believe Jesus Christ is the only way to find that deliverance... I know a lot of people in recovery, but I can't think of one who has done it without Jesus...
—Miranda

And now, we come to the end of the journey. It began as a lark, as party time, as a get together with a couple of so-called friends, as a trip down the yellow brick road, as a journey that promised an escape from current problems. Instead, it quickly turned into a tumble down the rabbit hole, and then it became an out-of-control free fall, that cost most people, more than they could ever have imagined. They lost money, jobs, homes, and saddest of all, shattered trust and broken relationships.

When we look at the causes, we can see and hear bits and pieces, hints of troubled lives, people looking in the wrong places for relief. They mistakenly believe the lie that drugs will somehow take away the stress, lessen the pain, or otherwise improve an already difficult situation.

Emotional issues, living in denial, I hid in my work... —Jean

Anything to escape, my parents fought constantly, they drank a lot... —Mark

My adoptive father sexually abused me from age 5 to age 12... —Lynn

There were already drugs involved in my life, whether I was doing them or not, with my mom's use, my dad's use, my boyfriend's use... —Karissa

My wife ended up cheating on me and I was so ashamed 'cause I thought it was my fault, I thought I wasn't man enough, I wasn't a good provider... —Jimmy

I just got out of juvenile hall. I wasn't very happy with myself. I wasn't happy with my family life. It had

nothing to do with my parents and everything to do with me... —Moses

I had no self-esteem. After I used, that's where I got my self-esteem... —Mary Ann

My parents got divorced when I was 11. I didn't have my dad around anymore, and I felt abandoned and I was very angry inside about that... —Justin

I was scared as a child. I was scared of everybody and everything... —Deanna

The reasons why they used drugs are as different as the individuals themselves, but for a majority of the respondents there were underlying factors. They told a story in no uncertain terms, that they were already unhappy and looking for something else to fill in the missing pieces of their lives. They thought, or were led to believe, that methamphetamine and other drugs might be a magic answer. Every one of them, as well as thousands of others across the Midwest and the entire nation, can now state unequivocally, that **meth is not the answer to anything except more misery and problems.**

Finally, as this journey draws to a close, we asked if there were anything else, anything these true experts on meth, felt had not been covered in the interview that they would like to share. Their final thoughts on methamphetamine, like their opinions on many other aspects of this journey, included an intriguing variety.

What were you not asked that should be covered in this interview that would be valuable in the fight against methamphetamine?

Meth is a living hell. It totally changed my character, changed who I was, changed all my morals, all my

outlooks on life. It changed my plans for the future. I had plans on going to college, and I barely got to graduate high school. I had plans on just so many things and it totally warped everything, caused me not to care, and asked me to hurt the people I love the most...
—Taryn

Parents need to take time to listen to their kids. Don't be a TV Mom or Dad. Don't be a let's-do-it-by-the-book Mom or Dad. We're all different. Just love 'em and take time to actually be there for them. Don't be peer pressured by the world... and if your kid is on drugs? Be there for them. Talk to them. Express how you feel. Communicate. Try to help them. No one understands a drug addict, that's what the drug addict thinks, when you're on drugs... —Russell

What parents can do to prevent [drug] use in their kids... kick 'em in the ass. I mean, they don't know nothing. They're eating Mom and Dad's food in the house. They need to intervene right there, hammer time. This soft love or whatever you call it, you love your kids and stuff, but if their son had a gun to his head and he's gonna shoot hisself, you're gonna jerk that gun out of his hand and take him down. He's doing the same. That child is doing the same thing, putting a gun to his head. They're gonna kill themselves or somebody else. It's gotta be hard. We gotta just jump up there and jump on top of people's cases, 'cause it ain't gonna be done by just being soft about it. It ain't gonna happen that way. It's gonna have to be done... everybody's gonna have to bite their lip, grit their teeth and go after it, because it ain't gonna happen any other way, unless they go in there full bore... —Russ

They have this idea that as soon as they can get you off the main drug that's killing you, that you're not addicted anymore. The thing is when you get into the

lifestyle of drug addiction; you're in a lifestyle of addiction. You need to be free from the addiction of drugs. You need to be delivered from sex addiction. You usually have, an addiction to foul language, the way you speak. You've got to be set free from that... I know people, they go from drug addiction to alcohol addiction, well, alcohol is the lesser of two evils and then they become alcoholics. You're not dealing with one addiction here, you're dealing with an addictive lifestyle, and all of these addictions have to be broken, not just getting off the one drug... you've got to transform, it's a battle of the mind... and if you're only dealing with one out of many addictions, then you're not really getting to the root issue, you're just treating a symptom... —Miranda

It's an addiction. All them years that I did it, 80 percent of the time, I wanted to be high. It made me feel like somebody that I wanted to be, that I wasn't. It made me feel like somebody better than I actually was. It gave me confidence in myself. I got a lot of work done when I was high... well, I probably imagined it, because you know when I came back from [Teen Challenge in] Michigan, I seen my house and I'm like, omigosh... My whole life was changed last year... —Lynn

You have to accept yourself as who you are. With the drugs, I used that to be somebody. I was a social chameleon. I don't have to be that today. What you see is what you get. Jesus loves us for exactly who we are and you don't have to try to be somebody you're not... —Mary Ann

I would like to say to anyone who is on drugs or who is contemplating suicide, I would like to let them know there is a heaven and there is a hell, and there is a consequence to what we do. I would encourage you... Give Jesus a try. Give him a try [because] I can say with all confidence, that without Jesus in my life today, I would not be who I am and where I am. I would be dead; physically dead without Jesus... instead I'm a full-time youth pastor... —Moses

My story's not complete and it won't be until my flesh takes its last breath. We're all a work in progress and it just takes making good decisions... The power of the Creator to change lives is being brought to the attention of those who doubt and are searching for ANY way to make life happen... Hundreds of stories are being heard and told regarding the only means of getting away from and out of bondage to addiction is through the power of God... EVERY person doing drugs wants to stop, even if they won't admit it. The opportunity to change life into something worthwhile is extremely attractive to someone who's been down and out for any amount of time... we need to teach people from the time they are children, that they are OK to be who they are, and they don't have to be any different. And they don't have to enhance artificially who they are as a person...Being OK with who you are, when you know who you are, when you're OK with who you are, you can say NO, and be OK with it... The lives of those recovered is astounding. The proof of the power of God is being seen in the evidence of changed lives. Mine is one of those changed lives... —Deanna

May you or your loved ones, or anyone you know or pray for, whose life has been impacted by methamphetamine, soon come to the end of the meth journey, so that all of you can begin the real journey of life, a life based on the loving mercy of Jesus Christ. That is where the truly glorious journey of life begins.

May you know and sense God's loving presence on every step of your journey. "**For God so loved the world that He gave his only begotten Son, that whoever believes in Him should not perish but have everlasting life**" (John 3:16).

DELIVERANCE

I woke up another day

Hazy eyes, lazy ways

Years and years wasting away, wasted today

I'm adding to this mixed-up world

Filling up with empty time

No directions

Just passing by

In whirlwinds of pointless and meaningless

I sought the answers

And in sweet temptations I tried them all

I've read the stars

Followed the paths of alien orbs

I was led to outer space

And lost sight in the black-hole of emptiness

I've held the crystals

Felt their inner energy

Adorned in beads and body-piercings

I listened in caves to the mighty crystallines

And followed them to depths of emptiness

I've heard the oracles

Cited the words of foreign doctrines

I've kissed their grounds and moved their motions

I swirled in the incessant yen

And spun around in patterned rings of emptiness

Ozark Meth: A Journey of Destruction and Deliverance

In whirlwinds of pointless and meaningless
I sought the answers
And in lavish emulation I tried them all
I've changed the chant, danced the dance,
I've shared the pipe and sought the vision,
I've spoken in tongues of words unknown
And I've bowed down to the demons below
I've held faith in worldly things
Even placed myself upon a mighty throne
It's a mixed-up world and I was free to fall
Sin to sin
I was part of them all
Sharing in only sinners' company
The devil's direction
End in sight
Rock bottom
Dead of night
And the sun went down
And the darkness grew
Time went bye
Deep within my rockened tomb
A heart beat

Deliverance

And the rumbling was felt
And the stone was moved
And on morning's light the rock rolled away
From out of the darkness there came a light
And on first morning's break the Son arose
A miracle to me came shining through
Reaching, grabbing ahold
A whisper
The most powerful of all,
"Here" He said. "This is for you."
And he spread his arms on the invisible cross
My God
He died for me
And I reached out
Salvation
And I claimed eternity
Blinding light
I embraced
And the Son arose

In His Presence, M. Jenn

A Final Testimony...

The following speech was written by Scott, the husband of one of the staff members of Intervention Ministries. It provides one last example of the journey on methamphetamine.

If you found yourself sinking in quicksand, and there were people all around you reaching out to help you out of the sureness of death that is slowly taking you under, would you not reach for help? Of course you would. Only an idiot would refuse.

It may shock you to know that many of you here tonight are sinking, struggling on your own to break free and refusing to acknowledge your need for help. The life is slowly being sucked out of you, so incrementally, it is barely noticeable. I'm talking about drug and alcohol addiction. And believe me; I know what I'm talking about. I spent 7 years in that quicksand. It is only by the grace of God that I stand here tonight, able to tell you about it.

I had a very normal childhood. My parents were responsible, honest people. We attended church for most of my childhood. There was no drug or alcohol abuse in my immediate family. I was a happy child, did well in school, and excelled in sports. After graduation from high school, I moved out on my own and was working when I started smoking pot and drinking. This was all new to me and I thought it was the greatest thing.

Over the next few years, I tried any drug that came along, acid, mushrooms, mescaline, speed, cocaine, you name it, I did it. It was the late 70's, and drug use was heavy. It was normal, or so I told myself, in an attempt to justify it; that was my belief.

I hadn't been to church in several years and my relationship with God was non-existent. I had a good job with a masonry company and was successful, making it to foreman in just 2 years. I lived to work and to party. But there was an emptiness inside of me. Something was missing. I grew very tired of the life I was leading, the endless hangovers from alcohol, the numbing of my senses from drug abuse. Then in the summer of 1980, I met Ronda. I knew from the moment I saw her that I would spend the rest of my life with her. I fell instantly in love with her and the feeling was mutual. I began to feel whole for the first time in years. On January 31, 1981, we were married and I felt like the luckiest man alive.

The drug use and drinking were habits that I continued, despite my wife's disapproval. Our daughter, Kristen was born in September 1981 and I was so proud. She brought us such great pleasure. I suddenly had a greater sense of responsibility. I was a happy, proud husband and father. The drug and alcohol abuse dwindled.

In 1982, we moved to Texas and I rented a house across the street from a Baptist church. The house had been their old parsonage and it wasn't long before we were invited to attend church. My wife was pregnant and she started to attend Sunday school and church. I told her it was fine for her to go but I was "too busy." Well, in her own sweet way, she talked me into going and I enjoyed it. There were a lot of young couples our age and we immediately made friends. I accepted Christ and was baptized. We lost the child Ronda was carrying in 1983, but in September, 1984, our son, Darren was born and life was good. I thought I had to be about the happiest man alive.

We stayed in Texas for several years and then in the summer of 1988, we moved to Missouri. We wanted

A Final Testimony

our children to grow up in a small town, like we both had. I didn't want to move them from school to school. We wanted to put down roots. We bought 70 acres with an old farmhouse on it, outside Humansville, where Ronda grew up. The masonry restoration company that I worked for had offices throughout the central United States, so I transferred to the home office in Fort Scott, Kansas. I hadn't used drugs in years and I rarely drank.

Our children grew and we were both involved in their lives. We coached ball teams, went to church on Sundays, went boating, fishing, hunting—we had a good life. I still remember the love we felt in that old house. The children were happy and Ronda and I were so much in love. I didn't think life could get any better than this. I felt complete.

In 1993, I was in a superintendent position at work and was doing quite well. In fact, I was second in job profit for the year. I was well respected on the job and in my community, as well as at our church. As I remember it, I was very tired one day at work and a co-worker offered me a line. Methamphetamine. I remember being scared to death. At that point, I hadn't done any illegal drugs for years. I despised them. I could tolerate people smoking pot around me as long as they'd didn't let me see them doing it, but chemicals were different. I had seen what happened to some of my previous co-workers and friends in years past, due to the use of chemicals like coke, heroin, and acid. I had developed a healthy distaste for them. Yet there it was, on a mirror in front of me and I guess, I gave in to peer pressure. I didn't want to seem square for some reason. What could one little line hurt? For an instant, I had a choice. The choice between right and wrong. I made the wrong choice, one that still haunts me and one that I still regret today.

The feeling of strength, exhilaration and euphoria was incredible. I admit I really loved the high. I found myself doing the drug as often as I could. I justified the use to myself because 'I only did it during the day at work.' The jobs were making a lot of money and the office commended me constantly for my hard work and dedication. The habit became daily and this went on for a couple of years. I would often hear about people being arrested for possession and manufacturing of meth and how addictive it was but I only laughed. A scheming ploy by law enforcement to scare the public, I thought. I mean, what could be so bad about this drug that enhanced my performance so much. I wasn't hurting me or my family or anyone else, for that matter. And it certainly wasn't the highly addictive drug that they were making it out to be. Little did I know at the time, that the drug was beginning to pull the veil over my eyes, blinding me to the destructive powers that were overtaking me.

I have to say, that my understanding of addiction, at that time, was non-existent. I had never really been addicted to anything. Addiction was, after all, something that happened to other people. What I came to learn, much later, is that addiction shows no bias. It destroys rich, poor, black, white, male, female, young, old, lawyers, auto mechanics, coaches, judges, athletes, politicians, and the list goes on. Nobody is exempt! But at this time, I didn't know any of these things and I sure didn't care.

My family life started to suffer. I was often late or a no-show at the kids games or after school activities. I broke promises. I began doing more and more of the drug. It was in 1995 or 1996 when I became friends with a guy who knew how to make meth, and I helped him for about a year. Needless to say, I had a lot of the drug now. I often went days without sleeping and when I did lie down at home, I would lie still in bed, awake all night, hoping my wife wouldn't notice how hard my heart was beating. I can remember many nights like that.

My work began to suffer immensely. I was late a lot. I'd lost about 30 lbs. and I didn't have the extra to lose. I thought I was doing fine but the jobs began to suffer and began losing money. I could tell when I went to the office that everyone wondered what was wrong with me, just by the way they looked at me. I was forced to step down from my Superintendent job and become a regular journeyman again. I had worked for the company for many years, and I know that is why they put up with me. News got around that I was into meth. I had been supplying several co-workers and people always talk. I was never confronted by my employer but things went downhill fast after that.

My wife rented a house in town for all of us, but the real reason was because she thought I was having an affair. I told her to meet me at the farm one day and I would tell her what was wrong with me. When I told her, she almost fainted. It just blew her away. We had been married for 15 years, had a beautiful marriage, two great kids whom I love with all my heart. We were involved with the community, church, kids' sports programs, and now this. I confessed to her. I was torn in two, because the addict in me was in control now, but down deep, the real me knew, I was in trouble. I loved my family and I loved meth.

I told her that I could kick it on my own, but I really knew that I couldn't. She wanted to believe me. One day she found a bag of meth in the old farmhouse, during deer season. I was hunting with my dad a few miles away, and I was walking back to my truck, when I saw her on the path. I couldn't believe she was in the woods without orange on! She showed me the bag, about 7 grams—I know because I had just weighed it the night before, when I made it. "What's this?" she asked and then she dumped it out. I went into a rage, yelling at her, to leave. After she confronted me, she saw my dad and told him and showed him the empty bag. I couldn't believe it! I couldn't believe she told him. I flew into a rage and made her leave so I could salvage some of the dope that was lying on top of the leaves. By now, I had a new addiction, making it. It fascinated me. I became bolder, going into stores and buying ingredients. I almost didn't care.

When it finally happened, I was arrested for possession with intent to distribute because I had so much of the drug in my truck. My wife and parents came and bailed me out. Of course, I promised them that I was done, that I would quit. They wanted to believe me, thinking surely after being arrested, I would wake up, but I just kept right on doing what I was doing. Somehow, I kept my job, but looking back, I don't know how.

I was convicted and sentenced to 7 years on a B felony, but because I had never been in trouble before, I did 120 days in a Department of Corrections treatment facility and was released on probation. Returning home, I had gained 40 lbs, and received a lot of compliments and encouragement from the people at church and at work. It was a few weeks before I went to see my old friend and sample his product once again. I hadn't learned anything. I hadn't learned to respect the addiction and never underestimate its power. I still didn't think the addiction thing applied to me. Besides, I held resentment towards the law. The amazing thing about addiction is, you never remember the bad times and you hardly ever blame the drug.

I had changed. I began to think evil and do evil. They call meth the Devil's drug and I can see why. My poor family's hopes of a recovered husband and father were shattered. I hardly ever came home anymore, just a couple of nights on the weekend. I didn't attend any of the kids' activities. I didn't do anything except work and cook dope. Every waking moment was consumed by gathering ingredients and manufacturing. My life revolved around that white powder.

In April 1998, I was arrested for possession. My wife had had enough. She didn't bail me out of jail this time. Looking back, I don't blame her. I finally talked my parents into bonding me out. I told them I was set up by the cops. As any parent would, they wanted to believe me. I had become such a habitual liar. I constantly found myself lying to everyone, to cover up my problem.

I begged and pleaded with my wife, to let me come back home and she finally gave in. I stayed at home more during the weekends, although I didn't spend time with them. I spent all of my time in the garage. I always had some pressing problem on a vehicle to keep me in my garage, where I could be alone, alone to do meth.

It's hard to explain. I love my wife and I love my children, but in reality, I loved my addiction more. Paranoia set in on me and I thought everyone who drove by was an informant. I covered all the windows in my garage.

In August, while I was waiting to go to court for the new possession charge, I was arrested again on my way home from Columbia where I had been working. I had a camper trailer that I parked in an RV park up there. I stayed in it and cooked dope all night, every night. I never slept during the time I spent in Columbia. One night on my way home, I had a trash sack full of remnants from my week's work. There was enough in the sack to convict me of attempt to manufacture, when I was stopped.

The 8 months between my last arrest and sentencing were a stressful time. I was completely out of control. Knowing I was going to prison this time, I tried to fit the most into the months of freedom I had left. A sane man would have wanted to spend time with his family, but I did the opposite. I had become such a habitual liar, always making up excuses about why I couldn't make it home. My old truck was constantly breaking down, or at least, that's what I would tell my wife. My sane self was tied up and gagged, unable to overtake the bully of an addict that had so forcefully taken control of my life.

When I went to prison, I weighed a sickly 137 lbs. My eyes were black and sunken in. I looked like a skeleton with skin. In the months following, I became severely depressed. Reality had set in and I knew it was going to be a long time before I would get out of prison. I had an 8-year B felony and a 7-year B felony, to be served concurrently. I sat there in that crowded, stinking prison, surrounded by men from every walk of life. It was a scary time. I had never really been to prison to do time. The 120 days I did in 1997 was just a small taste of what it was really like. That had been a scare tactic as much as anything else, one that didn't work.

I spent two months in Fulton's Reception & Diagnostic Center and from there; I was transferred to western Missouri prison at Cameron. It was there that I was hit with the brunt of prison life. The noise seemed relentless, more drugs than you can imagine, homosexuals everywhere. It's a reality of prison life, men who have spent much of their lives in institutions. The need for sexual fulfillment eventually leads many of them into this sick lifestyle. I watched young men arrive, boys more or less, ages eighteen to early twenties. The older ones would eye them with desire, much like a man would look at a woman, and the game is on. They would strike up a friendly conversation, then offer the deal. Drugs, they would front them drugs until the kid would be in debt to the point, he couldn't possibly pay. It was then they would be given the ultimatum, pay up or you will move in with me and be my boy. The tougher ones would put up a fight, only to be subdued. The smaller ones just gave in. Before long they got used to it, turned out, as they call it. If an owner owed somebody else, he would let them have his boy for a night or a week, whatever was necessary to pay off the debt. I have never in my life been in the middle of more evil than I was there. I was overwhelmed by it. I had my friends. We stayed to ourselves and minded our own business. I was lucky. I was older and I didn't appeal to them. I didn't use drugs; although not a day went by that I wasn't approached. I knew better than to get involved in that game.

It was soon after I was locked up that I realized if I wanted happiness back in my life, I needed Christ. As the fog of my addiction wore off, I realized just how badly I had screwed up my life, and how much pain I had inflicted on my wife, my children, my parents, and my friends. I was devastated as the reality of what lay ahead became apparent to me. I got on my knees and pleaded to my Lord for sanity, for strength and to honestly, change my heart. I felt it. I knew that He heard me and suddenly, I just knew that if I put him first and followed him, my life would not be a waste—that all of what I was going through would mean something! I remembered the verse Romans 8:28 "For we know that all things work together for the good for those who love God and are called according to his purpose." I realized that no matter how ugly, bad, or devastating something is, that God and only God can turn it into something good, wonderful, fulfilling. It was then I began to work at obedience, and becoming aware of the guidance of the Holy Spirit.

The two years I spent in prison were the hardest part of my life. At the same time, I grew more as a child of God in those two years than in any other time of my life. I know now that if this whole horrible experience had never happened, I would never have been humbled to the point of submitting to the authority of God's will for my life.

I tell you this in hopes that my story might spare one of you from making that wrong choice and destroying your life.

Scott wrote the above testimony in the Spring of 2001, while on work release from Ozark Correctional Facility at Fordland, Missouri. He was re-united with his family at that time. For two and a half years, he remained in sobriety, with a fire in his soul for the new life he had found in Christ. He also returned to masonry preservation work.

On August 15, 2003, while driving home from a job in northern Missouri, he was killed in an automobile accident. His legacy lives on, however, in his two grown children, Kristin and Darren, and his widow, Ronda. Ronda found this testimony amongst his things, after his death. It was the courageous decision of Ronda, Kristin, and Darren to share Scott's story here to warn others about the dangers of methamphetamine.

So What Do We Do Now?

Hey Mom, Dad...

You 'member that time last year
When you found Mark's syringe in my binder?
Thanks for believing me. But, it was mine.
You remember during Basketball practice
When Coach was yelling...
He had found that vile of crystal
On the locker-room floor?
Yep, it was mine.
Well, actually it was Jordan's and Katie's too...
We went in on it together.
See, here's the deal. Ya'll love us.
And we know that.
And ya'll want to believe us.
And we know that. You hear me?
We know you believe us.

But, well, we're experimenters,
And we're out to Experience anything and everything.
And, we're invincible.
We prove this to ourselves. And to our friends.
If we pull through a bad high, we get to brag about it.
'Course this raises the next high.

Bad thing though, if we don't pull through...

Well, we're just dead.

Yeah, bad deal.

Friends will cry

And whisper short-term warnings among themselves.

Parents will cover their ears, shut their eyes,

Close their mouths, shake their heads...

And think to themselves, "We never knew."

Mom, Dad, YES, YOU DO.

You know my friends. GET THIS...

If MY FRIENDS are getting grounded...

For pills, weed, pipes, powders,

Crystal, alcohol, smokes, syringes....

And these are my best friends...Did you hear me...

These are my best friends...

WHERE DID YOU THINK I WAS?

And now the last question remains, what do we do now? That, of course, depends on who you are and your current situation. If you have read the preceding chapters, and listened carefully to the people there who have told you their stories, then:

If you are a parent... grandparent, aunt, uncle, teacher, or anyone else who regularly has contact with children or teens. Help them to become self-confident young people, who have faith in God and faith in themselves. First of all, we all need to raise our children in church and encourage them in activities that will keep them as close to God as possible. While the vast majority of our respondents tell us, it is God who got them out of the world of meth, and keeps them out, they also agree if they had never wandered so far from God in the first place, they would not have ended up in the meth culture to begin with.

If your church does not offer adequate child/youth programs, then change churches or get involved with more than one. Find a church with active youth programs. Nearly every community (or neighboring community) in America has multiple churches or healthy Christian programs available, like the YMCA, Girls & Boys Town, Teen Challenge and others. Check out the national groups on the Internet. If there is absolutely nothing like this in your community, look into what it would take to start one! If it distresses you that there are no such programs available, there are very likely other parents in your community who feel the same way.

Meanwhile, look for ways to enhance a child's self-esteem. There are literally thousands of ways to help this process, from the advice seen on posters, such as *100 Ways to Praise A Child*, or to simply take the time to listen and encourage a child daily. Let him or her know that what they see and feel and think, is important. So many of our respondents made it clear that they had very little faith in themselves. They allowed themselves to try meth and other drugs that very first time, because they didn't want to appear lacking in some way in front of others. Whether they characterized it as wanting to fit in, not wanting to be left out, not wanting to appear square, wanting to be cool, it all came down to the same thing—they allowed others to influence a decision that had life-threatening consequences, because they did not view themselves as a person of value. No matter the age, a person who believes in themselves as a valuable child of God is not going to dump drugs or alcohol into their system.

We need to teach our children "you are worth it", not in terms of the latest Wall Street advertising campaign, but in terms of don't sell yourself short. You are worth so much more than the supposed "fun" these addictive substances supply. You are worth so much to God that He sent His Son, Jesus to die for you. You are worth so much to me, that I cannot imagine my life without you!

We need to continue to educate our children about the dangers of drug and alcohol abuse. We need to acknowledge the fact, that in the beginning, drugs do appear to provide some fun, or an escape from whatever problems you are grappling with at that moment. That short-lived escape, however, comes with a terrible price tag. And make no mistake; our children do grapple with some heavy pressures and problems. Even if we look back and think, gee, those days weren't so bad, that was a lot easier than dealing with what I struggle with now. Whatever your problems may be—a no win budget, lack of money, a difficult boss at work, a heartless landlord, no vehicle or one that barely runs, relationships that never seem to work right, parents or children with whom you never see eye-to-eye, whatever our problems are as adults, to young people, their pressures and problems are more overwhelming to their young systems and experiences. Take the time to acknowledge that.

Take the time, too, to literally, rehearse and role play, how a child might be approached to try drugs or alcohol. This may sound silly or awkward, at first. Even so, thinking about it beforehand, rehearsing what might be said, and more importantly, what they can say to refute the offer, perhaps without losing a friend, can be life-saving. Many times a youth may quickly find he or she does not walk away alone. Others, who are afraid to speak up, can and often will follow in the footsteps of one who leads them in the right direction, away from harm.

We also need to make certain our children understand there will be hard times in their lives. There will be times when they are desperately unhappy, depressed, hurt, angry, exhausted, or disappointed. Those times will come and they will go. In our add-water-and-stir instant society, many look for a quick fix to these feelings and that is another way that drugs and alcohol creep into their lives. We need to teach them to get through tough times by working hard, not giving up, and having faith that things will get better. Those lessons may very well make the difference, when they are faced with a difficult decision down the road.

If you are the relative of someone already addicted to meth...

Get Help Now! You may or may not be able to get your grown spouse, parent, child, or best friend to seek the assistance they need, but find help for yourself in the meantime. That was why Al-Anon was formed so many years ago as a part of Alcoholics Anonymous, for the family and friends of those struggling with alcoholism. The same applies to those who love someone addicted to meth. Find the support you need locally through churches, Alcoholics Victorious, Celebrate Recovery, Footprints, Alcoholics Anonymous, or other addiction groups. If you cannot find what you need locally, check out the Internet sites of these national organizations to find the group closest to you.

Whatever you do, get yourself and any children involved, to a place of safety. People who use meth regularly are sometimes violent. They tend to hang out with untrustworthy individuals. Anyone involved in the manufacturing of methamphetamine, presents a danger to themselves and all who live with them, as well as their neighbors and their neighborhood. There are many helping professionals in your community, from local law enforcement to those who work in mental health and your local health department who will lend a helping hand, if you ask.

While many people tend to view local law enforcement as the people who only come with handcuffs in hand, remember, these are the agencies who have been dealing with the plague of methamphetamine longer than any others, and most have a significant compassion for those involved. There are very few officers who have not had a relative or good friend of their own involved on the wrong side of the law. A concerned relative can call and get information. Many jails and probation offices keep a list on hand of active treatment centers who serve area residents. Remember, too, that if a person has been actively involved in selling or manufacturing methamphetamine for any length of time, local law enforcement is probably already aware of their activities, even if they have as yet, had no interaction. Informants and those already arrested have probably already shared their name with local drug officers. Most significantly, note that several of our respondents in looking back, now credit their arrest, with saving their lives. Sad as it is at the time, sometimes, that is what it takes to save a life.

If you are addicted to meth or any other substance...

Know that you are loved! That is the point of this whole book, to reach out to you and those who love you. We want to help you find your way back to a life that reflects that love. You are loved, by God, who sent His Son to die for you. His name is Jesus. You can read about Him and everything He did and said in the first four books of the New Testament. They are known as the Gospels, or the Good News— Matthew, Mark, Luke and John. You can also talk with others about Jesus and how He can reach out to you in your life— wherever you are, in a deep dark hole, in jail, it does not matter! Jesus will come into your heart, if you ask Him. No matter where you are, no matter how much trouble you've been in or are still in, Jesus will come to you when invited.

If you want to learn more about Jesus, reach for your nearest Bible or ask to talk to the chaplain or Jail Minister wherever you might be. There are other professional pastors and lay pastors, men and women who work in the community and serve as pastors on the side. They are committed to helping in the name of Jesus and you can find them in your community. Call or check your local churches, missions, or community centers, to find these friends. If you are concerned that the pastor of a local church might not understand your situation, call the local jail and ask to talk to their jail chaplain or Bible teacher. It's a guarantee that you cannot shock him or her or tell them about a situation where they cannot help you to find your way out. You have to be willing to do your part, however, and turn your life over to Jesus. All things are possible with God. That's Scripture (Mark 10: 27). It's also a fact. Go back and read it from the people who know, the people whose stories are told in this book. Get in touch with your local addiction support groups, Alcoholics Victorious, Celebrate Recovery, Footprints. You can find them through your local churches. They will help you break the bonds of addiction and stay in sobriety, free from the bondage of addiction, free to have a real life, full of love and happiness.

If you are a professional in a service profession...

Please note what are respondents have told us all in their own accounts. They have told us that addiction begins not with a gateway drug, but with a gateway person or two. It is in not wanting to look foolish in front of others, and in not having the strength to stand up for themselves, that the vast majority here, first tried methamphetamine or other drugs. It also has to do with the company they keep. All of our respondents echoed the words of one man who told us, he had to "find a new playground and new playmates" to break the addiction and stay in sobriety. Everything they told us here confirms there is no magic gateway drug that leads people down the road to methamphetamine. While drugs and alcohol were involved in many cases beforehand, they were not the classic gateway drug often sought by those studying addiction. It is also interesting to note that the majority of our respondents use tobacco in one form or another. While tobacco use has continued to increase in selected groups—youth, women, and minorities—its use has declined over the past several years in the general population. Exactly what this means in terms of addiction and possible personality traits is yet unclear, but it is definitely worth notation.

It is more than coincidental, that of the thirty people interviewed here, 28 told us in no uncertain terms that it was Jesus Christ and His Love that got them out of meth and keeps them out, to this day. That helps to explain why so many government rehabilitation programs have such a poor recidivism record, since they lack that key element. How government will ever come to terms with that remains to be seen, but it is obvious that faith-based programs are succeeding where those outside the faith, are not.

Finally, please do not fail to note the dynamic, energized lives that have been saved and are now coming into full fruition on the right side of methamphetamine. On the days when you feel overwhelmed by your caseload or depressed by the lack of progress of some of your clients, go back and read the words of our respondents, people like Deanna, Mary Ann, Russell, Meredith, Mark, Miranda, and Moses, just to name a few. They are all working every day to help others.

So What Do We Do Now?

They have suffered the worst ravages of methamphetamine and have come through it. They are a powerful 'give back army'; reaching back to pull others out of this sausage grinder that destroys lives. They are positive, encouraging, intelligent people who are contributing to our world everyday and we would not want to imagine a world without them.

Please keep them and all who are addicted, in your prayers and know that there are no hopeless cases. We know. We've seen it with our own eyes. With God, All Things Are Possible. Never Give Up. Tomorrow, you may be speaking with the next Deanna, Mary Ann, Russell, Meredith, Mark, Miranda, Moses or any one of thousands of others who still have so much to contribute. We need them in our world. Don't forget to PUSH—Pray Until Something Happens. And with God, know that something always will. God Bless you all!

Signs & Symptoms of Meth Use

- Rapid speech
- Ears ringing
- Voiding body waste
- Passing out
- Heart races irregularly
- Rapid jaw movement
- Translucent skin
- Misses work frequently
- Equilibrium problems
- Dry or itchy skin
- Poor bathing habits
- Brittle hair
- Impaired judgment
- Blurred vision
- Hallucinations
- Nose bleeds
- Euphoria or dreamlike stage
- Nose flesh eaten
- Menstrual cycle

- stops
- Loss of fetus
- Paranoia
- Phobic disorders
- Numbness
- Fidgeting
- Dehydration
- Kidney problems
- Biting finger nails
- Picking at skin
- Bloody scabs
- Rapid weight loss
- Can't eat days, weeks
- Sniffing excessively
- Spending tons of money
- Can't drink days, weeks
- Chest pain
- Panic attacks
- Hypertension
- Aggression
- Extreme fatigue
- Extreme sex drive
- No sex drive
- Dilated pupils
- Anxiety
- Nightmare
- Acne
- Tooth grinding
- Lives in seclusion
- Seizures
- Obsessive lying
- Strokes
- Slurred speech
- False sense of motivation
- Morals, values diminish
- Pushes away friends, family
- Dizziness
- Gazing or blank stare
- Extreme sweating
- Enamel on teeth rot
- Irritability

Appendix 1

"On Thin Ice"

We, at Intervention Ministries, are not the first to listen to those addicted to methamphetamine and attempt to put what we've heard down on paper. In 1999, Drs. Paul Thomlinson and Joseph Hulgus of the Burrell Behavioral Health Center of Springfield, Missouri, along with Todd Daniel M.A., Roger Ray D. of Ministry and Ray Radtke, did a year long study, interviewing and questioning 32 methamphetamine users, 20 females, 12 males, ranging in age from 24 to 44. There were some differences in approach, such as the more clinical methodology used by the Burrell Behavioral Center study to collect and process information. The ensuing years have rendered some data to be woefully outdated (the number of meth labs found in the area, for instance in 1999), however, the end results are incredibly similar.

Like those whom we have interviewed, they found methamphetamine use to extend across a wide range of individuals. Their group included 19 percent who had not finished high school, 31 percent who had some college education or degree, and even one individual with double bachelor's degrees. Another 22 percent were employed in managerial or clerical jobs or were college students.

They determined that despite the fact that most who eventually go on to use methamphetamine, first experimented with alcohol, tobacco, and even in many cases marijuana, the "true gateway is not another drug, but is people. The drug spreads associationally through relationships with other users and existing relationships with using friends and family, and continues for a variety of complex interpersonal reasons... the present research suggests that methamphetamine use spreads relationally. Most of the respondents indicated they began use in the presence of friends and sometimes family. They were introduced to the drug by those around them and consequently introduced others to the drug. Romantic relationships were also a source for many of the females who used when their boyfriends asked them to."

Drs. Thomlinson and Hulgus and their colleagues go on to say that "perhaps too little is said in the discussion of methamphetamine about the positive effects of the drug. Obviously, our respondents did not choose this drug specifically because they wanted to lose their teeth, become a human skeleton, or be arrested. Something lures them to use, and that something is a promise of the drug. Whatever the drug offers (and immediately supplies) is more powerful than the external deterrents which restrain use.

What was their first focus of perceived benefit from trying the drug? Some were pushed by painful childhood experiences, aided by repeated exposure to all types of drugs through immediate and extended family. Perhaps most importantly, methamphetamine had two emotional benefits: it manufactured a feeling of competence and invulnerability and it blunted negative feelings they did not wish to feel. The initial experience therefore, became tremendously rewarding and exceptionally reinforcing. More than just blunting painful, negative emotions, methamphetamine manufactured extremely positive emotions to replace the original pain."

This study also found that family dynamics are very strong factors related to first time use, as 41 percent of their respondents cited social or family motivations in their responses to questions regarding their initial use. "It is difficult to overestimate the role of family in methamphetamine use and addiction: 47 percent of participants got their supply from an intimate or relative. Nearly all (94 percent) revealed that methamphetamine had disturbed or broken their family relationships, including loss of children and severing ties with parents. Finally, a quarter of respondents (26 percent) indicated that family might have been a protective factor for them—if they had known how to intervene, if they had shown appropriate caring and education and the like."

Seventy-eight per cent (78 percent) of the respondents in their study reported that methamphetamine use improved their performance in their work or other physical activities. Furthermore, 48 percent stated they believed that meth use had enhanced their sexual performance; however, 92 percent of those who made that statement were male, while only 2 out of 20 women made the same claim. "It may be significant to note that a substantial number of respondents expressed the notion that all manner of performance enhancements are more apparent than real when using." One participant who felt her creativity was stirred by her drug use said, *'I wrote a lot of stories and such and threw them all away—they didn't make any sense when you read them after the high was gone.'* Another put it this way, *'Meth enhanced what I was doing—but only in my head.'*

Despite its perceived benefits, most also found there were other factors that soon outweighed whatever good they thought they might have found in the use of methamphetamine. Respondents' listing of side effects included:

68 percent who referred to paranoia in statements, like "*I thought people were trying to steal my dope*" or "*I feared someone would break into my house*";

48 percent who made reference to hallucinations, such as "*I would see mice on the floor and not step on the floor by moving two chairs and stepping on them*";

35 percent who described various physical effects, such as rashes or the shakes;

32 percent who made note of aggressive or hostile behavior;

29 percent who reported irritability, and

16 percent talked about confusion or memory problems.

Nearly half, 43 percent of those in the Burrell study, spoke of having lost a job, some even an entire business, as a result of their meth use. Another 30 percent stated that they had quit before they were terminated or they left their job because 'selling [dope] was easier'. Overall, a total of 73 percent of those involved in this study, found their work to have been negatively impacted by their use of methamphetamine. A significant 37 percent stated that they had not lost their job and claimed that their use of the drug had actually improved their ability to function, at a higher level.

A number of the participants in this study reported receiving medical treatment for a variety of ailments associated with methamphetamine use. They included:

"*Problems with bleeding sinuses. One reason I went to IV was to save my nose*";

"*Not able to breathe well; it was like my body was shutting down*";

"Pneumonia, pleurisy, and bronchitis—I would get run down—my lowest weight was 108 pounds at 5'10";

"I thought my heart was going to explode out of my chest, and I had chest pains I attribute to meth use. I had dental problems, I lost all my teeth";

"Been to the ER twice in the past year for bronchitis I believe was due to meth use. I've also had severe kidney and bladder problems I feel are due to the chemicals in meth";

"My overdose, suicide attempt, kidney failure, dehydration, and hypothermia".

When asked about the impact on their family, only 2 of the 30 respondents in the study denied that there had been any significant effects on their family life. Of those remaining, 57 percent stated that meth had indeed disturbed or strained life within the family. Another 47 percent were classified as broken families. Half of whom lost custody of their children, at least for a time, as a direct result of their use of meth.

The final question asked by the Burrell study was intended to broaden their study and bring more respondents into the participant pool, when they asked, "Do you know any methamphetamine users who haven't been involved with the legal system, or haven't been in treatment, who might agree to do this confidential anonymous interview?" They received only one affirmative response. The 30 other responses were not only negative, they also cited the paranoia common to many meth users, and included the following comments—*'Hell, no. Ain't gonna happen. Secrets keep you alive!' 'I don't know any current users that will talk to you—the paranoia thing.' '... Don't hang around those people anymore'. 'I wouldn't invite them up here because they're scummy people'* and finally, *'I don't really know—most are in jail—there's not too many left.'*

More than five years after this initial study of methamphetamine users in the Ozarks, the general consensus amongst users remains the same, in terms of outcomes for those who use. What has greatly changed and increased are:

The numbers of clandestine labs found by law enforcement;

The numbers of arrests of methamphetamine users, dealers and manufacturers;

The growing financial burden placed on public services from hospitals and burn units, to social service and law enforcement agencies, due to methamphetamine abuse;

The number of people still trying and using the drug;

And the human wreckage in terms of lives, homes, families and children threatened, damaged or destroyed, because of the use of methamphetamine.

Appendix 2

What The Numbers Tell Us

On the following pages are the results of the first questionnaire presented to all thirty of our respondents *before* their in-depth interviews. The main purpose of these questions was to help the individuals put their personal story in order, literally, to organize their thoughts about their life experiences as related to meth. The results, however, gave some other hints and indicators in reference to those who use methamphetamine.

For instance, while many assume that those who abuse illegal drugs have had an unusually difficult childhood, several of these questions indicate that the majority of our respondents:

Grew up in families with both a mother and father present in the home (80 percent)

Came from families of average or above average financial status (90 percent)

Had appropriate responsibilities within the family as children and teens (90 percent)

Were supported in their endeavors while growing up (67 percent)

Were average or above average students (80 percent)

Were high school graduates (67 percent)

Continued their education past high school (53 percent)

Consider themselves overachievers (67 percent)

None of the above items point to neglected children, or adolescents who were abused or mistreated, although certainly there are individual cases that include those aspects.

Some information shared here shows our respondents to be exactly in the middle of things, so to speak.

Was there a divorce situation? (50 percent)

Did your brothers and sisters use drugs? (50 percent)

Did you move a lot in your formative years? (50 percent)

Were you and your siblings treated and supported equally? (53 percent)

Were you disappointed by a teacher or other adult while growing up? (50 percent)

Again, nothing in the above, gives any indication as to why some reach for methamphetamine and other drugs, while others in the same age group, do not.

Finally, there are a few questions that indicate some areas may be a more pivotal influence in the choice to use methamphetamine.

Was there drug/alcohol abuse in the family? (60 percent total, 69 percent males)

While growing up, were there other family members involved in drug or alcohol abuse? (70 percent total, 75 percent females, 62 percent males)

Statistics: What The Numbers Tell Us

How old were you when you first tried a controlled substance/alcohol? (74 percent total did so at ages 11-15; 82 percent females, same age, 61 percent males, same age)

Do you use tobacco products? (69 percent)

While the above statistics do not give any iron-clad rules as to who may or may not use meth in the future, they certainly point to some areas of similarity that bear closer scrutiny. Certainly, according to these figures, the use of alcohol and tobacco seem to make it easier for many people to push on to the next step of illegal substance abuse.

Other factors also require more attention. For instance, a majority indicate they attended church prior to their use of methamphetamine (64 percent). After their experiences with meth, 97 percent claim a renewed, stronger faith is an important part of their life today.

A great many questions remain, and there are many ways to analyze the answers we have already received. Statistics may come and go. Their analysis will always be a primary fascination to some, less profoundly convincing to others.

Life's most profound changes, however, take place in the context of meaningful relationships. The way out of methamphetamine use is the same as the way in—relationships. Spending time with the wrong people will end in wrong choices. Correspondingly, spending time with the right people will transform life in the right direction. This is the relational impact that meth survivors have found in Jesus and His followers. Life in Jesus Christ offers so much more than life in meth. Ask any of our thirty survivors. They'll be glad to tell you about it, statistics notwithstanding.

SOUTHWEST MISSOURI DRUG TASK FORCE ANALYSIS

Thirty respondents, 17 female and 13 male, completed the survey on July 1, 2005. All responses shown are percentages.

No.	Question	Response	Total	Female	Male
1	While growing up, were there a mother and father in your home?	Yes	80	81	77
		No	20	19	23
2	Was there a divorce situation?	Yes	50	56	46
		No	50	44	54
3	Was there a step-parent?	Yes	43	44	46
		No	57	56	54
4	What was your family's financial status?	Above average	43	41	46
		Average	47	53	39
		Below average	10	6	15
5	Was there physical, verbal or mental violence directed against you or a sibling, or between your parents?	Yes	63	62	62
		No	37	38	38
6	Was there drug or alcohol abuse in the family?	Yes	60	50	69
		No	40	50	31

No.	Question	Response	Total	Female	Male
7	At what age should drug education be taught to children?	Under age 5	23	24	23
		Elementary school	71	76	61
		Middle school	3	0	8
		High school	0	0	0
		Unanswered	3	0	8
8	Did your brothers or sisters use drugs?	Yes	50	56	46
		No	40	32	46
		Unknown	10	12	8
9	At what age did your brothers or sisters use drugs?	Not applicable	37	41	31
		Ages 5–10	3	6	0
		Ages 11–15	30	29	30
		Ages 16–20	17	12	23
		Ages 21–26	3	0	8
		Over 26	0	0	0
		Unknown	7	12	0
		Unanswered	3	0	8
10	What drugs did your brothers or sisters use? *Includes (but not limited to) acid, cocaine, marijuana, meth, pills*	Not applicable	37	41	31
		Combination of Drugs	57	53	61
		Unknown	3	6	0
		Unanswered	3	0	8

No.	Question	Response	Total	Female	Male
11	If not, why do you feel they didn't? Includes (but not limited to) followed parents, saw what I went through, maturity, goal-oriented, responsible, liked staying out of trouble	Not applicable	50	58	38
		Unknown	13	6	23
		Drinks alcohol	3	0	8
		Active in sports	3	6	0
		Combination of Reasons	24	24	23
		Unanswered	7	6	8
12	Do you think your brother or sister would be willing to allow us to interview them on this matter?	Yes	40	38	46
		No	40	50	23
		Unknown	20	12	31
13	While growing up, were any of your family members involved in abuse of drugs or alcohol?	Yes	70	75	62
		No	30	25	38
14	Was there a death or separation in your family due to violence, drugs or alcohol abuse?	Yes	47	44	54
		No	53	56	46
15	Was corporal punishment used in your family?	Yes	47	56	38
		No	47	38	55
		Unanswered	6	6	7
16	What area were you raised in?	City/outskirts	37	29	46
		Small town	37	47	24
		Rural	13	12	15
		All over the place	13	12	15

No.	Question	Response	Total	Female	Male
17	Did you move a lot in your formative years?	Yes	50	50	45
		No	50	50	55
18	Were you given responsibilities commensurate with your age (chores, room clean up, etc.)?	Yes	90	87	92
		No	10	13	8
19	Were you supported in your endeavors while growing up?	Yes	67	63	69
		No	30	37	23
		Unanswered	3	0	8
20	Were you and your siblings treated and supported equally?	Yes	53	50	62
		No	43	44	38
		Unanswered	4	6	0
21	Are you a high school graduate? *(GED: 4 females, 1 male)*	Yes	67	56	77
		No	33	44	23
22	Did you continue your education?	Yes	53	56	54
		No	47	44	46
23	What sort of student were you?	Above average	37	53	15
		Average	43	35	54
		Below average	20	12	31
24	Were you bullied school?	Yes	23	13	31
		No	77	87	69

No.	Question	Response	Total	Female	Male
25	Were you a bully in school?	Yes	27	25	23
		No	73	75	77
26	Were you disappointed by a teacher or other adult in your formative years?	Yes	50	50	54
		No	50	50	46
27	Did you serve in the military?	Yes	7	0	15
		No	93	100	85
28	What is your family status?	Married	33	35	31
		Single	11	18	0
		Separated	13	18	8
		Divorced	43	29	61
		With children	66	75	54
		No children	14	19	8
		Unanswered	20	6	38
29	Are any immediate family members using drugs?	Yes	37	37	38
		No	63	63	62

No.	Question		Response	Total	Female	Male
30	How old were you when you first tried a controlled substance or alcohol?		Ages 5–10	13	0	31
			Ages 11–15	74	82	61
			Ages 16–20	10	18	0
			Ages 21–26	0	0	0
			Over 26	0	0	0
			Unanswered	3	0	8
	Average age:	*12.7 years*				
	Female average age:	*14.1 years*				
	Male average age:	*11.3 years*				
	Youngest age for female:	*11 years*				
	Youngest age for male:	*6 years*				
31	What did you first try?		Alcohol	47	47	46
			Acid, meth, pot	3	6	0
			Cigarettes	3	0	8
			Alcohol, cigarettes	3	6	0
			Pills, cigarettes	3	6	0
			Marijuana	34	35	31
			Unanswered	7	0	15
32	How old were you when you first tried meth?		Ages 5–10	0	0	0
			Ages 11–15	10	6	15
			Ages 16–20	47	52	38
			Ages 21–26	27	24	31
			Over 26	13	18	8
			Unanswered	3	0	8
	Average age:	*20.4 years*				
	Female average age:	*21.1 years*				
	Male average age:	*19.8 years*				
	Youngest age for female:	*13 years*				
	Youngest age for male:	*14 years*				

No.	Question	Response	Total	Female	Male
33	How many times did you try to get off and failed?	0 attempts	13	0	23
		1–6 attempts	27	23	31
		7–12 attempts	0	0	0
		Over 12 attempts	57	71	38
		Unanswered	3	0	8
34	How did you use methamphetamine?	Ingest, smoke, snort	10	18	0
		Inject	10	12	8
		Inject, pills, smoke, snort	41	46	31
		Inject, pills, snort	7	6	8
		Inject, smoke	3	0	8
		Inject, smoke, snort	7	6	8
		Pills, smoke, snort	3	0	8
		Pills, snort	3	6	0
		Smoke, snort	13	6	21
		Unanswered	3	0	8

No.	Question	Response	Total	Female	Male
35	How have you been off methamphetamine?	Under 1 year	47	41	54
	Average time off: 2.5 years	1-5 years	33	47	15
	Female average time off: 2.2 years	Over 6 years	17	12	23
	Male average time off: 2.8 years				
	Female longest time off: 10 years				
	Male longest time off: 12 years				
	Female shortest time off: 2 weeks				
	Male shortest time off: 1 month				
36	Are you off all drugs?	Yes	97	100	92
		No	0	0	0
		Unanswered	3	0	8
37	Do you use alcohol?	Yes	20	19	23
		No	77	81	77
		Unanswered	3	0	7
38	Do you use tobacco products?	Yes	67	69	69
		No	30	31	24
		Unanswered	3	0	7
39	Do you gamble?	Yes	7	0	15
		No	90	100	78
		Unanswered	3	0	7

No.	Question	Response	Total	Female	Male
40	Do you consider yourself an overachiever or underachiever?	Overachiever	67	76	54
		Underachiever	10	6	15
		Unknown	7	6	8
		Neither	13	12	15
		Unanswered	3	0	8
41	Are you employed?	Yes	77	75	84
		No	20	25	8
		Unanswered	3	0	8
42	Has the use of meth caused you to lose a job?	Yes	66	75	54
		No	27	19	38
		Unanswered	7	6	8
43	Did you attend church prior to using meth?	Yes	64	63	62
		No	23	19	31
		Unanswered	13	18	7
44	Does faith play an important part in your life now?	Yes	97	100	92
		No	0	0	0
		Unanswered	3	0	8
45	Have you been arrested for using meth or other drugs?	Yes	67	63	69
		No	30	37	23
		Unanswered	3	0	8

No.	Question	Response	Total	Female	Male
46	Have you been arrested for offenses not drug-related?	Yes	50	38	61
		No	47	62	31
		Unanswered	3	0	8
47	Did law enforcement treat you fairly?	Yes	60	56	61
		No	20	13	31
		Unanswered	20	31	8
48	Did the courts treat you fairly?	Yes	67	63	69
		No	13	6	23
		Unanswered	20	31	8
49	Should either have been harder or easier on you?	Easier	13	12	15
		Harder	16	18	15
		Neither	40	41	40
		Uncertain	7	0	15
		Not applicable	17	29	0
		Unanswered	7	0	15
50	Who do you admire most?	Mother	13	22	0
		Father	13	12	14
		Mother and father	7	12	0
		Grandmother	7	12	0
		Daughter	7	6	8

No.	Question	Response	Total	Female	Male
	Who do you admire most (continued)?	Brother	3	0	8
		Honest people	3	6	0
		Any martyr	3	0	8
		No one individual	3	6	0
		Unanswered	10	0	23
51	What is your happiest memory? *Multiple answers include (but not limited to) camping in the mountains, finding biological mother, 'now'*	Not receiving a life sentence	3	6	0
		Birth of child	34	34	31
		Turning my life over to God	20	12	31
		Marriage and children	13	18	8
		Multiple answers*	20	24	15
		Unanswered	10	6	15
52	What is your saddest memory?	Abortion or rape	7	12	0
		Losing custody of child	10	12	8
		Getting a real look at myself shooting up	3	6	0
		Realizing I was spiritually dead	3	6	0

No.	Question	Response	Total	Female	Male
	What is your saddest memory *(continued)?* *Multiple answers include (but not limited to) spouses' adultery, divorce, causing pain to parents, mothers stroke*	Going to jail or prison	7	0	15
		Lab explosion or jail	3	6	0
		Multiple answers *	17	12	23
		Death of family member or someone close	40	46	31
		Unanswered	10	0	23
53	What are your strongest qualities? *(The 30 individual answers were compiled into these groupings for statistical purposes)*	Determined, dependable, hardworking	43	47	38
		Love people, honest, kind, soul-saving	33	29	38
		Positive, encourager, sense of humor	10	12	8
		Leadership, imagination	7	6	8
		Unsure or unanswered	7	6	8

No.	Question	Response	Total	Female	Male
54	What are your weakest qualities? *(The 30 individual answers were compiled into these groupings for statistical purposes)*	Motivation, responsibility, self-esteem	27	35	15
		Peer pressure, permissive, fear, behavior	27	29	31
		Lust, temper, authority, food, alcohol	13	12	15
		Reading, writing, spelling, education	3	0	8
		Opinionated, bossy, whiny	27	24	23
		Unanswered	3	0	8

About the Authors

Laura L. Valenti of Lebanon, Missouri is a 10-year veteran of the Laclede County Sheriff's Department in southwest Missouri, where she and her husband have lived for the past 25 years. For the last 3½ years she worked at the Sheriff's Department, she was the Jail Administrator, running the county's 106-bed facility. It was during this  time particularly that she was hit with the full force of the meth epidemic in her home area.

Valenti is also a volunteer on the board of New Life Jailhouse Ministries. This Christian ministry operates a transitional house for area women coming out of jail or prison. New Life staff and volunteers work to help empower women to learn the skills they need to function in society, without drugs or other addictions.

Valenti is a former Peace Corps volunteer in El Salvador, where she worked in education and community development. While working as a feature writer for her local newspaper, she wrote her first book, *The Fifteen Most Asked Questions About Adoption.* She continues to work as a freelance writer, and a Spanish/English interpreter and translator.

She and her husband, Warren, are the parents of four grown children, three of whom they adopted from El Salvador and the U.S. She is an active and founding member of Journey Christian Church (Disciples of Christ) of Lebanon, Missouri, which was established in May 2000.

 **Dick Dixon** has lived in Bolivar, Missouri for the past 30 years. A native of southern Illinois, Dick has a Bachelor's degree from Southern Illinois University and a degree from Southwest Baptist University of Bolivar. He is an ordained gospel minister.

The father of three daughters, Dick Dixon and his family spent 10 years working as tribal missionaries among the Aria and Ivanga tribes in Papua New Guinea. He speaks three languages and was also trained as a medical technician for his work in New Guinea. The Dixon family came to Bolivar, Missouri as cattle ranchers and Dick still calls his cattle operation, his hobby.

Intervention Ministries was founded in Bolivar, Missouri in 1994 by Dick Dixon and family, where he has worked with individuals in crisis intervention for the past 11 years. The work of Intervention Ministries is to meet a person at their point of need and frame a Biblical perspective of life for the individual. Dick knows personally that Christ is the turning point for change over any addiction. Under his direction, Intervention Ministries is seeking the power of sustained change for the methamphetamine addict. *Ozark Meth: A Journey of Destruction and Deliverance* is one more facet of that work.

Need More Help?

To obtain additional copies of this book, please contact Intervention Ministries on the Internet at:

www.interventionministries.com

Our web site offers links to other organizations and assistance in fighting addiction to methamphetamine.

Or you may write or call us at:

315 N. Albany
Bolivar MO 65613
Tel. 417-326-7352

METH TAKES AWAY EVERYTHING